Other Clarion books by
JIM MURPHY

The Indy 500

Death Run / *A Novel*

★ ★ ★ ★ ★ ★ ★ ★ ★ ★ ★ ★ ★ ★ ★ ★ ★

BASEBALL'S

JIM MURPHY

★ ILLUSTRATED WITH PHOTOGRAPHS ★

CLARION BOOKS
TICKNOR & FIELDS: A HOUGHTON MIFFLIN COMPANY
NEW YORK

For Charlie Hess — with special thanks
for all your good advice and support

Clarion Books
Ticknor & Fields, a Houghton Mifflin Company
Copyright © 1984 by Jim Murphy

All rights reserved. No part of this work may be reproduced or transmitted in any form or by any means, electronic or mechanical, including photocopying and recording, or by any information storage or retrieval system, except as may be expressly permitted by the 1976 Copyright Act or in writing by the publisher. Requests for permission should be addressed in writing to Clarion Books, 52 Vanderbilt Avenue, New York, NY 10017.
Printed in the U.S.A.

Library of Congress Cataloging in Publication Data

Murphy, Jim, 1947–
Baseball's all-time all-stars.

Includes index.
Summary: The author presents two hypothetical "all-time, all-star" teams chosen from the best players in baseball history, with accompanying research to support his choices.
1. Baseball players — United States — Biography — Juvenile literature. [1. Baseball players]   I. Title.
GV865.A1M85   1984   796.357′092′2   [B]   83-14977
ISBN 0-89919-229-7

Designed by Victoria Hartman

Q 10 9 8 7 6 5 4 3 2 1

Acknowledgments

The author would like to thank the following individuals and organizations for their valuable and generous assistance in rounding up information and photographs: Howard C. Talbot, Jr., Director, and Donna L. Cornell, Photographic Department, National Baseball Hall of Fame and Museum, Inc.; Mr. Lou D'Ermilio, Public Relations, The New York Yankees; Mr. Richard L. Bresciani, Director of Publicity, The Boston Red Sox Baseball Team; Ms. Sharon Pannozzo, Assistant, Public Relations, The Chicago Cubs; The Baltimore Orioles; The Detroit Tigers; The New York Mets; The Atlanta Braves; The Cincinnati Reds; and The Pittsburgh Pirates.

Photo Credits:

The National Baseball Hall of Fame and Museum, Inc.: 8, 20, 25, 28, 44, 53, 64, 68, 93, 97, 98, 102; The New York Yankees: 60, 76, 106; The Baltimore Orioles: 72, 110; The Chicago Cubs: 12, 40; The New York Mets: 28, 54; United Press International: 48, 72; The Boston Red Sox Baseball Team: 86; The Pittsburgh Pirates: 17; The Detroit Tigers: 82; The Atlanta Braves: 35; Associated Press: 39, 68.

Contents

INTRODUCTION   1

A WORD ABOUT STATISTICS   4

THE TEAM ROSTERS   5

THE NATIONAL LEAGUE TEAM   7

THE AMERICAN LEAGUE TEAM   59

BUT WHAT ABOUT . . .   114

BIBLIOGRAPHY   115

INDEX   117

Introduction

The idea of this book is basically very simple—I've assembled two teams of the very best players in professional baseball history. The players I selected were judged on their all-around game, hitting, run production, base-running, and so on, with particular attention to how they played their position in the field. I've tried to highlight some of their extraordinary skills and tell what physical and mental qualities helped them to perform at such a consistently high level.

Because over 13,000 men have played in organized baseball since 1876, I've set guidelines to maintain order and fairness in the selection process.

First, subtle rule variations, particularly in the location of the strike zone, make hitting and pitching in the National League different than in the American League. I decided the best solution was to choose a team from each league and not try to compare and contrast players to form a single "best" team.

Second, the physical and mental demands of playing in the field vary with the position. Therefore, I grouped players by the position they played most in their career, and I judged them only against others at that position.

Third, statistics are the lifeblood of any baseball fan because just about everything a player does can be translated into numbers. And stats are helpful in evaluating a player's performance, which is why this book has its share of numbers. But statistics can often be misleading. An example will illustrate this.

The highest lifetime fielding percentage for every position, including pitcher, is held by players whose careers began after 1950. Does this mean that modern players are better fielders than those from earlier decades? Not necessarily. There have been a great many improvements in equipment and in the playing field itself that give modern players an advantage defensively. The oversized basket glove extends a modern player's reach considerably. Astroturf and better ground maintenance have made the modern field smoother so the ball doesn't take as many bad bounces. I've tried to figure in these (and many other) factors when comparing players from different eras.

To make these comparisons, I've had to consult numerous baseball histories and encyclopedias, personal recollections, biographies, and so on. In the case of pitchers, I've tried to evaluate the quality of the team they pitched for. Cy Young won more games (511) than any other pitcher in baseball history, but he didn't make the team. Although he happened to play for some very good ball clubs, he managed to lose a record 313 games and have very erratic ERAs from season to season. While a superstar, Young lacked consistency.

Fourth, I've played down the importance of World Series and All-Star game appearances and performance, as well as awards such as Most Valuable Player, Cy Young Award, Golden Glove Award, and even induction into the Hall of Fame.

Getting into the World Series is never an individual achievement; it's a team effort. And playing in All-Star games and the Series is distinctly different from normal, everyday play. Ty Cobb managed to come away with an incredible .367 batting average for twenty-four years of play. Yet, his World Series average in seventeen games is an unimpressive .262.

Almost all the awards are, to varying degrees, based as much on a player's popularity as his skill. When I do mention such awards, it's usually to point up a player's consistency. For instance, Bob Gibson won the Golden Glove Award nine times in a row, despite being a rather surly fellow. Obviously, the voters of this award didn't give it to Gibson because of his personality!

My aim in setting these ground rules was to give every player an equal and unbiased shot at making the teams. Even so, I'd be foolish to think my selection process was perfect. Choosing only Major Leaguers automatically excludes outstanding athletes from the more than seventy-seven countries around the world that play professional baseball. Worse, it leaves out super baseball players from the Negro Leagues, such as Satchel Paige, Buck Leonard and Judy Johnson. It's not that information isn't available on these players, though it is often sketchy and in some cases incomplete. The biggest problem is in evaluating the level of competition they faced.

I stuck with the Major Leagues exclusively because at any time in its history its players were the best in the world. Period. I believe the players in *Baseball's All-Time All-Stars* represent the very best of the best.

A Word about Statistics

You can't have baseball or books about baseball without including a lot of statistics. And every year new ways are invented to evaluate a player's performance — game-winning hits, batting average with men in scoring position, pitching records according to months, and so forth. I've included what I consider the most important and accessible statistics and left out the more arcane ones. The abbreviations appearing in statistics column following each player's and pitcher's section are as follows:

Players

G	= Games played	R	= Runs scored by player
AB	= At-bats	RBI	= Runs batted in by player
H	= Hits	BB	= Bases on balls
2B	= Doubles	SO	= Strikeouts
3B	= Triples	SB	= Stolen bases
HR	= Home runs	BA	= Batting average

Pitchers

W	= Wins	IP	= Innings pitched
L	= Losses	H	= Hits allowed
G	= Games pitched in	BB	= Bases on balls allowed
GS	= Games started	SO	= Strikeouts
CG	= Complete games	Sho	= Shutouts
Pct	= Pitcher's winning percentage		
ERA	= Earned run average per nine innings		

Relief Pitching

W	= Wins	SV	= Saves
L	= Losses		

The Team Rosters

The National League   7
First base: Bill Terry   9
Second base: Rogers Hornsby   13
Shortstop: Honus Wagner   16
Third base: Pie Traynor   21
Right field: Stan Musial   24
Center field: Willie Mays   29
Left field: Hank Aaron   33
Catcher: Johnny Bench   37
Pitcher: Grover Cleveland Alexander   41
Pitcher: Christy Mathewson   45
Pitcher: Sandy Koufax   49
Pitcher: Bob Gibson   51
Pitcher: Tom Seaver   55

The American League   59
First base: Lou Gehrig   61
Second base: Eddie Collins   65
Shortstop: Joe Cronin   69
Third base: Brooks Robinson   73
Right field: Babe Ruth   77
Center field: Ty Cobb   83
Left field: Ted Williams   87
Catcher: Bill Dickey   91
Pitcher: Eddie Plank   95
Pitcher: Walter Johnson   99
Pitcher: Lefty Grove   103
Pitcher: Whitey Ford   107
Pitcher: Jim Palmer   111

THE NATIONAL LEAGUE TEAM

☆ | FIRST BASE | ☆
BILL TERRY

William Harold Terry (Memphis Bill)
Born: October 30, 1898, Atlanta, Georgia
Career dates: 1923–1936   Hall of Fame: 1954
Batted and threw left-handed

What motivates grown men to play baseball year after year? The reasons and the intensity of those reasons vary, of course. Some simply love the game. Others crave the competition or the limelight. Bill Terry's inspiration for playing, and playing well, was money. More than anything else he wanted to be rich.

Terry's obsession with money was probably a by-product of his youth. He grew up in a poor section of Atlanta with few prospects of ever escaping it. At age thirteen he dropped out of school to work. "When I was fifteen," Terry recounts, "I was doing a man's job, loading sacks of flour from freight cars." He married at eighteen, and was a father a year later.

Terry loved baseball, and played the game after work whenever possible. He even spent two years playing the outfield for a minor league team, though he quit to take a better-paying job for Standard Oil in Tennessee. While playing for the company team, he was noticed by the New York Giants. His meeting with Giant manager John McGraw, however, gives some idea of what came first for Terry.

"How would you like to come to New York with me?" McGraw asked, assuming any red-blooded American kid would beg for the opportunity to play with his World Champion team.

"What for?" the twenty-three-year-old Terry asked.

"To play with the Giants, maybe."

"For how much?"

"Do you understand what I'm offering you?" McGraw sputtered. "I'm offering you a chance to play with the Giants—if you're good enough."

"Excuse me if I don't fall all over myself, but the Giants don't mean a thing to me unless you can make it worth my while."

The Giants eventually made it worth Terry's while. And his playing was worth every penny he was paid. The Giants moved Terry from the outfield to first base, and he immediately applied himself to mastering the new position. After spending two years at the Giant farm club to improve his fielding, followed by two slow years in the majors, Terry emerged as a team star in all categories.

During the next twelve years, Terry batted well above .300 eleven times, finishing with a .341 career average, second only to Rogers Hornsby for National Leaguers and thirteenth best of all time. And he regularly collected over one hundred runs and RBIs a season. His 1930 season saw him hammer out 254 hits (second only to George Sisler's 257), 23 homers, 139 runs and 129 RBIs. His average that year was a league-leading .401.

In the field he moved swiftly and gracefully, which was surprising because he was six foot one and weighed a little over 200 pounds. He lacked the blazing speed of other players, but he had quick lateral moves and an uncanny instinct for knowing where the ball would be hit. In all, he led the league in assists and putouts five times and fielding average four times. His career fielding average is an impressive .992.

Exactly what part money played in Terry's continued success in the field and at the plate is hard to determine. What is known is that he asked for and received raises each year — and his play never faltered. When he was thirty-seven, Terry banged out 203 hits for a .341 average.

Some people considered Terry's attitude crass and greedy. Baseball was a sport, not a business, they contended. Always demanding more money detracted from the game's beauty and purity. Others, especially more modern players and writers, see Terry as hard-nosed but smart. He was, after all, playing at a time when there was no union to protect players. Club owners dictated contract terms, and either the players accepted or they didn't work.

Terry's exit from baseball was provided in 1932 when he was appointed manager of the Giants. He played and managed for five years (hitting .350, .322, .354, .341, and .310), then retired from play to manage another four years. Terry left baseball in 1941 after managing the Giants to three pennants and amassing some very solid statistics. And maybe even a little more important to Terry, he left the game a millionaire.

G	AB	H	2B	3B	HR	R	RBI	BB
1721	6428	2193	373	112	154	1120	1078	537

SO	SB	BA
449	56	.341

Rogers Hornsby (right) with teammate Hack Wilson

☆ | SECOND BASE | ☆
ROGERS HORNSBY

Rogers Hornsby (The Rajah)
Born: April 27, 1896, Winters, Texas
Died: January 5, 1963, Chicago, Illinois
Career dates: 1915–1937   Hall of Fame: 1942
Batted and threw right-handed

"It don't make no difference where I go or what happens," Rogers Hornsby once said, "so long as I can play the full nine." And that's the bottom line on Hornsby: he loved baseball with a passion.

This was true from his earliest years growing up in Winters, Texas. He was always out somewhere playing baseball, often late into the night. As a minor leaguer, he studied the game carefully, hitting techniques in particular. Oddly enough, however, it was his sparkling glove work that earned the nineteen-year-old a spot with the St. Louis Cardinals in 1915.

Hornsby's pro career started slowly. His first season average was an anemic .246. Even when he topped .300 in three of the next four years, he showed little power. Then Cardinal president Branch Rickey encouraged Hornsby to gain weight. At the time, Hornsby weighed only 140 pounds. During the following off-season, Hornsby worked on a farm and managed to add forty pounds to his frame.

In 1920 Hornsby's hitting exploded. That year he collected 218 hits, 44 doubles, and 20 triples and averaged .370 at the plate. But this was just a warmup for one of the greatest five-year hitting sprees in baseball history. Hornsby's 1921–1925 averages were .397, .401, .384, .424, and .403 (an average of .402 for five years and all league-leading numbers).

During this stretch, he led the league in hits and doubles five times, triples once, home runs twice, runs three times, and RBIs four times. He dominated National League hitting so completely that sportswriters began referring to him with the title of an Indian prince, "The Rajah."

His play in the field equaled his hitting ability, and many consider him the finest fielding second baseman of his time. He was very fast, had sure hands and a strong, accurate arm. He ranks twelfth all-time in assists with 5166 and helped turn hundreds of double plays. And his .957 lifetime average is exceptional considering he played before the oversized basket glove was introduced.

Yet even as he sparkled in the field and at the plate, a darker side of his personality began to emerge. He often turned moody for no apparent reason. He refused to hang around with his teammates, and he quarreled constantly with management. When he was made manager of the Cards in 1926, his often tactless remarks to his players alienated him from them further. As one writer bluntly put it, "he was irascible, moody, petty, irritable, the last man you'd invite to a party." Not that Hornsby would go if you did invite him. He rarely went to social gatherings. He didn't even go to movies, fearing they would damage his eyes and his hitting ability.

After managing St. Louis to a World Championship in 1926, Hornsby demanded a three-year contract and was abruptly traded to the New York Giants. The fans in St. Louis were in an uproar. But as Rickey explained: "I have shown a forgiveness almost divine toward this player. I have overlooked the unspeakable names he called me. . . ." The St. Louis management had simply had all they could take of Hornsby.

Hornsby continued his quarrelsome ways for three consecutive years, going from New York to Boston to Chicago. And yet through all these unsettling moves (complicated by several lawsuits), he managed to play superb ball, hitting .361, .387, and .380.

It seemed as if "The Rajah" would reign forever, but he was injured sliding into third in 1930. After this, his playing time was sharply curtailed, though his belief that he was above management and baseball rules wasn't. He was fired from his last job in 1937 because he refused to comply with a league rule forbidding players from gambling on horse races.

When he left, his career average stood at .358, second only to Ty Cobb's. But if people thought Hornsby was through, they were greatly mistaken. He joined a semi-pro team in 1938, then organized the Rogers Hornsby Baseball School. He even managed and played for several minor and Mexican league teams into his mid-fifties. There's little doubt about it: Rogers Hornsby may have had his problems with people, but he loved to play baseball.

G	AB	H	2B	3B	HR	R	RBI	BB
2259	8173	2930	541	169	301	1579	1584	1038

SO	SB	BA
679	135	.358

☆ | **SHORTSTOP** | ☆

HONUS WAGNER

John Peter Wagner (The Flying Dutchman)
Born: February 24, 1874, Carnegie, Pennsylvania
Died: December 6, 1955, Carnegie, Pennsylvania
Career dates: 1897–1917   Hall of Fame: 1936
Batted and threw right-handed

When a young Honus Wagner trotted out to replace the Pittsburgh Pirates' popular shortstop Bones Ely, the crowd at the game booed. Who was this awkward-looking kid anyway?

Their initial reaction was understandable. Wagner stood a squat five feet eleven inches tall, was noticeably bowlegged, and weighed around two hundred pounds. In addition, his arms were so long that pitcher Lefty Gomez once quipped that Wagner was the only person he knew who could tie his shoelaces without bending over.

The simple fact was that Wagner looked more like an ungainly bull than an athlete. And yet Wagner took his physical attributes, and through constant practice, made himself one of baseball's greatest all-around players.

The first thing people noticed about Wagner was his speed. He seemed to be rolling along instead of running, but he was much faster than he appeared. He managed to lead the league five times in stolen bases and his career total of 722 is fifth highest ever. He was so successful on the base paths that sportswriters began referring to him as "The Flying Dutchman," forgetting that Wagner's family was from Germany.

16

His quick acceleration and speed helped him in the field as well, giving him surprising range. He was especially skilled at going into the "hole" between short and third when the third baseman couldn't handle the ball. When his speed left him just shy of a hot grounder, his long arms and big hands gave him the extra inch needed to snag the ball. And Wagner got to the ball a lot during his career, totaling 11,626 chances, the seventh greatest number in baseball history.

"He didn't seem to field balls the way we did," a fellow teammate once said of Wagner. "He just ate the ball up with his big hands, like a scoop shovel, and when he threw it to first you'd see pebbles and dirt and everything else flying over there with the ball."

He may have lacked fielding grace, but he got the job done. Wagner is second all-time in putouts for a shortstop with 4891 and fifteenth in assists at 6056. He was such an exceptional fielder that the manager of the rival New York Giants, John McGraw, was heard to grouse, "The only way to get the ball past him is to hit it eight feet over his head."

Wagner even managed to look out of place while batting. He'd stand deep in the box, hunched over, his bat wiggling in anticipation. When the ball arrived, he'd lunge at it, usually slapping a screaming line drive to the outfield. Wagner's enormous power came from working first in a coal processing mill, then in a steel mill while growing up in Carnegie, Pennsylvania. His eye for the ball came from taking batting practice after games whenever he could get someone to pitch to him.

The results are some impressive hitting stats. He took eight batting crowns and led the league in doubles eight times and in triples three times. He's sixth on the all-time hit list, third in triples, and fifth in doubles. Both his runs and RBI totals rank among the top fifteen, and he hit above .300 for seventeen consecutive years! His lifetime average of .329 is impressive for any player, but remarkable when you consider the pounding his body took on the base paths and at shortstop.

Yet for all of the acclaim Wagner received as a player, he remained a quiet, shy, and humble man off the field. Of his hitting, Wagner's only comment was, "I guess I hit pretty fair."

He shunned publicity and remained loyal to Pittsburgh even when other clubs offered him more money. Wagner also refused to cash in on his fame.

Once a Pittsburgh scorer, John Gruber, was offered ten dollars (a good sum in those days) if he could persuade Wagner to allow his picture to appear on a cigarette pack. Wagner refused, but felt bad that a friend might suffer financially because of his decision. Wagner sent Gruber this letter: "Dear John, I don't want my picture [associated with] cigarettes, but I don't want you to lose $10, so enclosed is a check for that sum."

Coexisting with this gentle off-the-field nature was one of baseball's most competitive players. Angered over the possibility of being walked intentionally, Wagner once leaped at the fourth ball and sent it to the wall for a double.

What Wagner did during his twenty-one-year career was create an individual style of play that worked for him. It was unteachable to anyone else simply because no one was built like him. In 1936, when the Baseball Hall of Fame inducted its first five members, Honus Wagner was one of them.

G	AB	H	2B	3B	HR	R	RBI	BB
2786	10427	3430	651	252	101	1740	1732	963

SO	SB	BA
327	722	.329

☆ | THIRD BASE | ☆
PIE TRAYNOR

Harold Joseph Traynor
Born: November 11, 1899, Framingham, Massachusetts
Died: March 16, 1972, Pittsburgh, Pennsylvania
Career dates: 1920–1937   Hall of Fame: 1948
Batted and threw right-handed

Harold "Pie" Traynor had an open, friendly personality. He was quick to lend a hand and easy to get along with. But when it came to fielding balls hit around third, few in baseball history could rival his fierce aggressiveness. His glovework was so brilliant that he spent only three months in the minors before the Pittsburgh Pirates brought him up in 1920 to take over at shortstop.

In his second season, Traynor was shifted to third (to make room at shortstop for the great fielding Rabbit Maranville) and immediately set about learning his new position. His reflexes and speed made this a relatively easy chore for him. His lateral movement was excellent, and he had an uncanny ability to anticipate where the ball would be hit. He was so good at going into the hole, he was sometimes referred to as "Pittsburgh's second shortstop."

His ability to cover huge amounts of ground allowed Traynor to play even with the bag most of the time. This was important during the era when Traynor played. There was no artificial turf then, just grass. A wily hitter could tap a slow grounder up the line that would die in the tall grass. If the third baseman played too deep, he'd never reach the ball

| 21

in time to throw out the runner at first. Traynor's positioning and speed let him scoop up these would-be hits effortlessly.

And Traynor got to a lot of these balls, ranking eighth all-time in chances at third with 6140. He ranks fifth in putouts (2291) and twelfth in assists (3525). Traynor was so effective at stopping the ball that most batters hit to the right side of the diamond rather than challenge Traynor.

One of Traynor's great strengths was his arm. When he came up with the ball, he threw quickly and accurately, even when off-balance. His quick arm helped him start four double plays in one game, a major league record. He ranks eleventh in this category with 308.

It's natural to wonder how Traynor stacks up to his counterpart in the American League, Brooks Robinson. A quick glance at the overall stats might lead some to assume that Robinson had it all over Traynor. But Traynor's career was much shorter — 955 games, to be exact. If you average out their fielding stats, Traynor is just about even with Robinson in chances per year, and he trails Robinson in assists and double plays by only small margins. And Traynor actually leads Robinson in average putouts per year. Most people who saw both third basemen play would give Robinson a slight edge in fielding over Traynor, though only a slight one. But Traynor has an obvious lead in hitting.

Traynor had strong wrists and eagle eyes. He regularly slapped out over 180 hits and over 20 doubles a season. He had 10 or more triples eleven times, a mark of his speed and daring base running. But Traynor's most impressive stat is his strikeouts. He averaged only 16 a year. That's a startlingly low number when you consider that Reggie Jackson strikes out over 120 times a season on average. In 1929, Traynor struck out just 7 times in 540 times at bat.

His .320 average is the highest for any third baseman. And his runs and RBI production were considerable and steady.

Traynor was made manager of Pittsburgh in 1934. He seemed on his way to combining managing with playing as Bill Terry and Joe Cronin did. Then, late in the year, Traynor injured his arm while sliding into home against the Phillies. After this, his arm lost its zip and his effectiveness at third decreased. He played sporadically in 1935 and 1936, then retired. He left the game as its best fielding and hitting third baseman ever.

G	AB	H	2B	3B	HR	R	RBI	BB
1941	7559	2416	371	164	58	1183	1273	472

SO	SB	BA
278	158	.320

☆ | RIGHT FIELD | ☆
STAN MUSIAL

Stanley Frank Musial (Stan the Man)
Born: November 21, 1920, Donora, Pennsylvania
Career dates: 1941–1963   Hall of Fame: 1969
Batted and threw left-handed

When Stan Musial played his last game in 1963, he walked away with an awesome bagful of National and Major League hitting records. Ironically, his career as an outfielder in baseball came about only because of a freak accident and Musial's own single-mindedness.

Stan Musial grew up in Donora, Pennsylvania, one of six children of Polish-speaking immigrants. He was a quiet kid, normal in every way, except maybe for his excessive love of baseball. When he graduated from high school, his parents wanted him to go on to college, but Musial stubbornly refused. Instead, he signed a pro contract (over his parents' objection) to pitch for the Florida State League.

In his three seasons there he posted respectable records of 6–6, 9–2, and 18–5. But he had control problems and wasn't regarded as a Major League prospect. Fortunately for Musial, his manager, Dickie Kerr, felt his young player might have more potential as a hitter than as a pitcher. He began playing Musial in the outfield. It was while chasing down a fly ball that Musial crashed to the ground, injuring his shoulder.

Any thoughts of a pitching career for Stan Musial (in the major or minor leagues) were gone. Many players would have

given up their plans to play pro ball right here, but Musial turned to learning how to hit with vengeance, putting in long hours at the batting cage. And he mastered hitting despite what had to be the oddest stance in baseball history.

Musial stood deep in the batter's box, his body twisted in an awkward-looking position, bat held high. His stance is frequently described as looking like a kid peeking around a corner. When the ball arrived, he uncoiled, lashing at the ball no matter where it was pitched.

Early on in his career, many baseball people predicted his stance would result in frequent slumps. But slumps rarely came, and never stayed long, mainly because Musial had a keen eye for the ball—his 1599 walks and low number of strikeouts attest to that. Musial batted over .300 for his first seventeen years in the majors, winning seven batting titles. He even managed to hit .312 in 1947 despite suffering from an inflamed appendix that had to be removed immediately after the final game.

Musial's career hit total is the fourth highest, while his lifetime .331 average ranks him twenty-fourth. He is second only to Tris Speaker in doubles, ranks twentieth in triples and fourteenth in homers for a total of 1377 extra-base hits. That's just 100 less than major league leader Hank Aaron.

In the field, Musial was swift enough to cover great chunks of territory and sure enough to glove most of what headed his way. He led the league three times in fielding average and was always near the leaders in this category, even when shifted to center field or first base.

Even more remarkable than his play was Musial's personality. In twenty-two years of major league baseball, he never seemed to exhibit ego problems or temperament. He never grabbed for the limelight, never became rude or abrupt despite the pressures of a tight pennant race. He remained accessible to fans and sportswriters. When he retired, he was probably the best-loved player in baseball. The combination of his personality and sparkling play was so outstanding that even opposing fans referred to him fondly as "Stan the Man."

G	AB	H	2B	3B	HR	R	RBI	BB
3026	10972	3630	725	177	475	1949	1951	1599

SO	SB	BA
696	78	.331

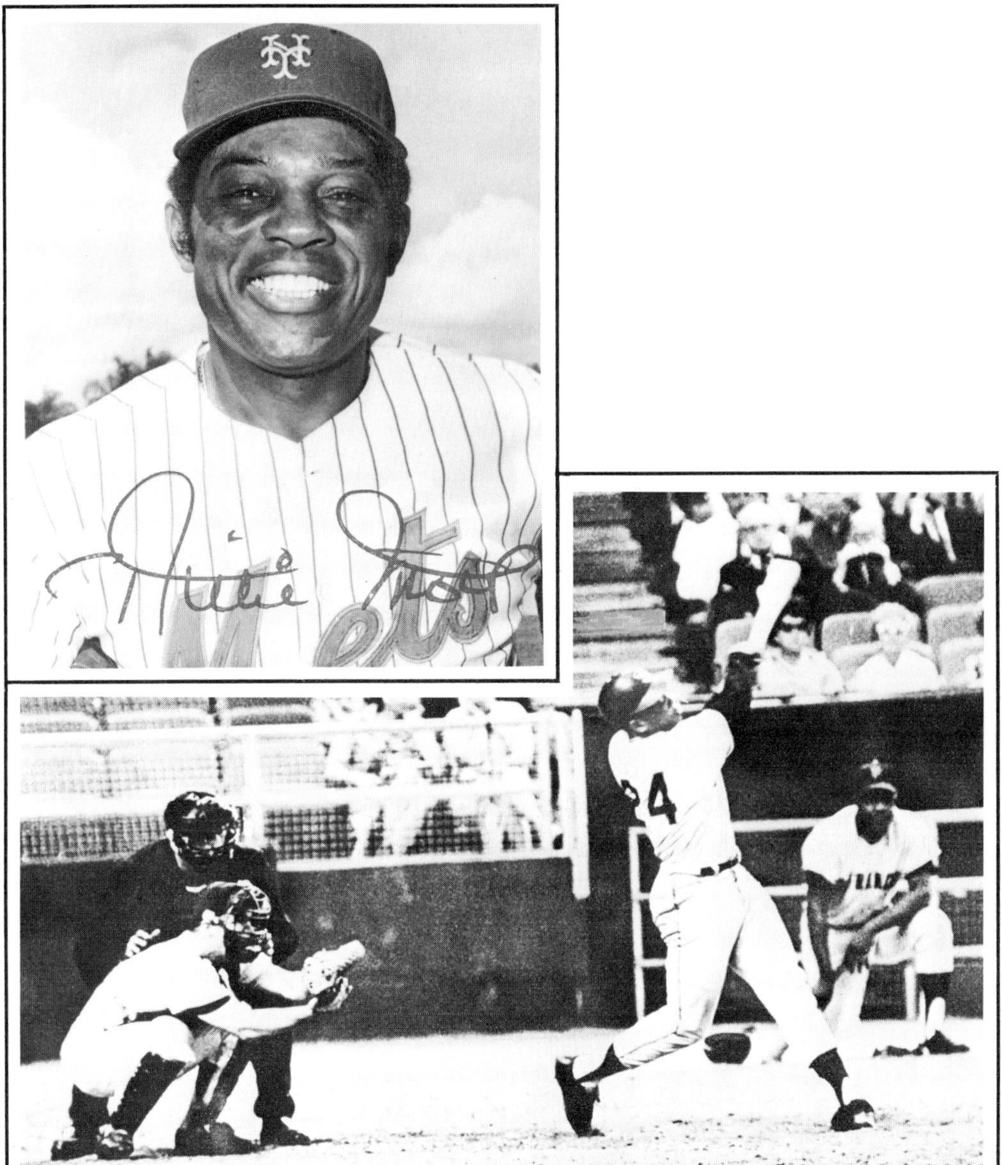

☆ | CENTER FIELD | ☆

WILLIE MAYS

Willie Howard Mays (Say Hey)
Born: May 6, 1931, Westfield, Alabama
Career dates: 1951–1973   Hall of Fame: 1979
Batted and threw right-handed

When Willie Mays was just three seasons into his major league career, he was already considered one of the best — if not the best — all-around players in the game. He hit for a high batting average and power. He ran bases with a daring reminiscent of Ty Cobb and roamed center field effortlessly. It was, in the words of Joe DiMaggio, as if Mays had been "born to play ball."

DiMaggio's statement was closer to the truth than he probably realized. From a very early age, Willie played ball constantly, receiving good advice on hitting and fielding from his father. When he was six, Willie would often hit high fly balls and then sprint to catch them himself!

He was a versatile athlete at Fairfield Industrial High School in Alabama, excelling in basketball, football, and baseball. But Mays's father steered his son toward baseball, possibly realizing that at five foot ten and a half and 170 pounds, Willie was too small for basketball or football.

At age seventeen, Mays broke into the Birmingham Baron's lineup in the Negro National League. But Mays wasn't destined to remain there long. In the wake of Jackie Robinson's historic and highly productive entry into the majors in 1947, scouts were already combing the Negro leagues for talent. The New York Giants contracted Mays and sent him to their Minnesota club for seasoning.

He was there two months and batted a conspicuous .477! He was simply too good for the minor leagues, so the Giants brought him up in 1951.

"What I marveled at," said fellow Giant Bill Rigney, "beyond his ability, was the instinct he had for the game. Mostly, you have to teach players a lot — even the ones who are tremendous athletes. But Willie seemed to have it all."

His first year average of .274, with 22 doubles and 20 home runs was good enough to earn him Rookie of the Year honors. He played only 34 games in 1952 before being drafted into the army. But when he returned to the Giants in 1954, he was even stronger than when he left. That year, he lead the league with a .345 average and blasted 41 homers, 33 doubles, and 13 triples.

It was his speed that set him apart from (and above) other players. He was one of the fastest men in baseball and had the quickest acceleration. Two or three steps and he was at top speed. His quickness let him turn what should have been an infield out into a single, and an outfield single into a double. And it was his speed that let him lead the league in steals four times (and this during a time when base stealing wasn't an important part of the game). Once when the Cubs' catcher let the ball dribble ten feet from the plate, Mays scooted home from third. Most players wouldn't have even tried to go from first to second on the play.

Speed was his ally in the field as well. He played most hitters in shallow center, confident that he could chase down anything that went over his head. Playing shallow allowed him to catch many weak pop flies that might have otherwise dropped in for hits. And playing shallow also set up some of baseball's greatest catches.

Everyone, it seems, has a favorite Mays catch.

Some point to his home-run-robbing stab of a Roberto Clemente blast, while others recall his daring catch of Ed Bouchee's sinking liner. And, of course, there was his spectacular over-the-shoulder nab of Vic Wertz's 500-foot drive in the 1954 World Series.

The wonderful thing is that Mays made such catches often and made them look routine. He seemed to do everything with the same spirit. His swing was so ferocious that often his cap would sail off. Even on routine flies he'd cruise under them and make his nonchalant "basket catch," as if to challenge the hitter to make the next one a bit harder to catch.

It was his energy and style that made him instantly popular with fans and earned him his nickname: The Say Hey Kid. But his cheery exterior concealed a brooding nature. He could suddenly turn moody and withdrawn for no apparent reason. He snubbed small-town reporters and treated fans with disdain. He demanded and usually got special treatment from his managers. And it was Mays who decided when he would practice and play.

But how could anyone refuse him? In 1952, when Mays played those first 34 games, the Giants had a 26-8 record and led the league. After he went in the army, the team nose-dived and lost the pennant. The fact was that when Mays was happy he played well; and when he played well, the Giants won. So Giant management tolerated his ego.

When he retired, Mays left with the third highest home run total, behind only Hank Aaron and Babe Ruth. He is fourth in career runs and seventh in RBIs. And he ranked eighth on the hit list and third in total bases with 6066.

Willie Mays was "born to play ball." What's more, he played each game as if the pennant were on the line.

G	AB	H	2B	3B	HR	R	RBI	BB
2992	10881	3283	523	140	660	2062	1903	1463

SO	SB	BA
1521	338	.302

☆ | LEFT FIELD | ☆
HANK AARON

Henry Louis Aaron
Born: February 5, 1934, Mobile, Alabama
Career dates: 1954–1976   Hall of Fame: 1982
Batted and threw right-handed

It was the first game of the 1974 season, with Cincinnati pitcher Jack Billingham facing Atlanta's Hank Aaron. Billingham ran the count to 3–1, then challenged Aaron with a sinking fastball. "It wasn't a bad pitch," Billingham would say after the game, "but it wasn't good enough against Hank Aaron."

Aaron's powerful wrists whipped his bat around and sent the ball on a line shot into the left-field seats. His first swing of the season and Aaron had hit home run 714, tying Babe Ruth's career mark. His pursuit of the most sought-after baseball record was almost over.

It was a quest that had begun modestly back in 1954 when Aaron took over in left field for the injured Bobby Thompson. His rookie stats were solid (.280 average with 13 HRs) but gave no indication of what would follow. During the next few years, Aaron's hitting would improve steadily. The 1957 season was vintage Aaron when he batted .322 and led the league in home runs (44), runs (118), and RBIs (132).

"In the next couple of years they'll be talking about Hank the way they do about Rogers Hornsby," said Atlanta Braves manager Fred Haney. "Hornsby's best power was to right center. This kid's got just as much there and more to other fields. He's one of those things that come along once in a lifetime for a manager."

Aaron's hitting ability came from his quick, strong wrists and amazing concentration. He could wait on a ball, following its trajectory to the plate, then snap his bat around to make contact. He could even take a pitch well out of the strike zone and muscle it into the seats.

Hitting ability was one thing, but matching Ruth's record of 714 home runs was something else entirely. Nine players hit more than 500 home runs, then faltered. Willie Mays was only the second player (besides Ruth) to reach 600, but age slowed his reflexes and he retired with 660. What Aaron possessed in addition to his bat was consistency and durability.

Aaron broke his leg in September of his rookie year, but had no other serious injuries for the rest of his twenty-three-year career. This allowed him to play in more games and get to bat more times than anyone else in baseball history. Aaron never dominated hitting categories the way Cobb, Ruth, Musial, Mays, or Hornsby did, but his yearly totals were always high and eventually added up. He holds the major league marks in home runs, total bases (6856), and RBIs. He's second in hits and runs, and seventh in doubles.

When Aaron reached age thirty-five, he was closing in quickly on the aging Mays's home run totals, with Ruth's record still in the distance. It was at this point that Aaron began an incredible finishing kick, hitting more homers between 1969 and 1973 than in any previous five-year span. He thumped out 44, 38, 47, 34, and 40, ending the 1973 season with a total of 713!

There's no way to measure the pressure on Aaron's shoulders during this final drive to break the home run record, though it had to be incredible. He received death threats

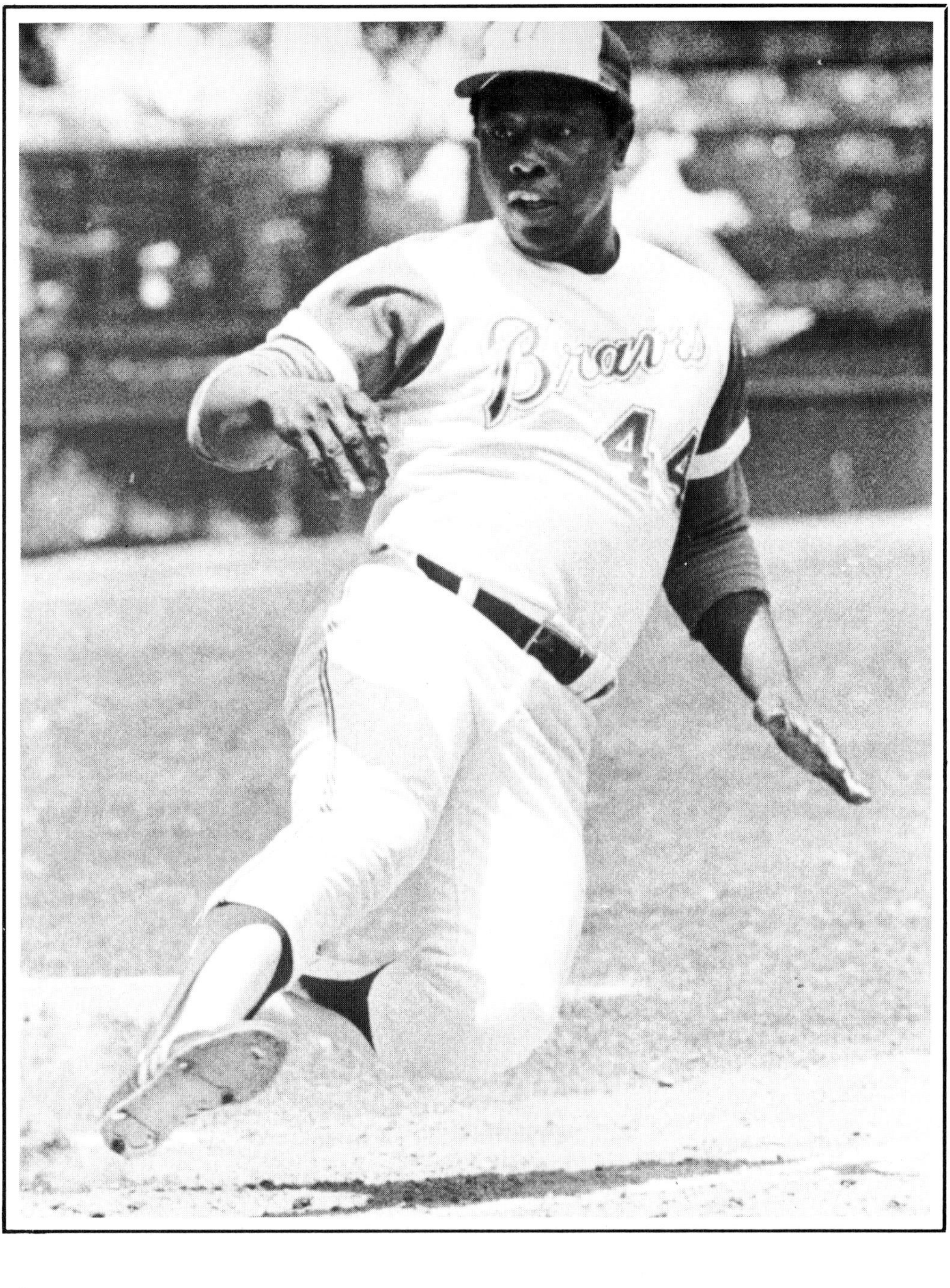

from people who didn't want to see the Babe's immortal record broken by a black man. Writers began comparing Aaron (and not always favorably) with Ruth. And then the commissioner of baseball, Bowie Kuhn, tangled with Atlanta's management to intensify the heat of the spotlight on Aaron.

The cause of this trouble was simply that the Braves wanted to hold Aaron out of the lineup so that he could hit the historic home run in Atlanta. Kuhn overruled the Braves' decision and ordered Aaron to play — and Aaron, ever calm, responded with his blast off Billingham.

"I never went on the field and failed to give anything but my best," Aaron would say later. "I don't know how to play the game any other way."

It was an attitude he carried with him in the field and on the base paths, too. His long, fluid strides let him gobble up lots of ground in the outfield as he chased down the ball. He had a sure glove, developed earlier in his career when he was an infielder. He even managed to steal bases when necessary. His stolen base totals look average, but they hide the fact that he got 203 of them in a single ten-year period.

Ultimately, and like Ruth, Aaron will go down in the books because of his home run hitting. Just a few days after he hit home run number 714, he faced Los Angeles's Al Downing in Atlanta. Downing threw a fastball and Aaron hit it on a line over the left center-field fence. As Aaron circled the bases, the giant scoreboard flashed the number 715. Aaron's quest for the record that had eluded so many others was at an end.

G	AB	H	2B	3B	HR	R	RBI	BB
3298	12364	3771	624	98	755	2174	2297	1402

SO	SB	BA
1383	240	.305

☆ | CATCHER | ☆

JOHNNY BENCH

Johnny Lee Bench
Born: December 7, 1947, Oklahoma City, Oklahoma
Career dates: 1967–1983
Batted and threw right-handed

All successful teams need a leader, someone who can take charge no matter what the situation, provide the spark that makes the difference between winning and losing. Johnny Bench was just that person for the Cincinnati Reds in the 1970s, when they won six division titles, four National League pennants, and two World Series.

Bench's take-charge attitude and confidence were evident even as a twenty-year-old rookie. "I'm not an excitable person," he has explained, "so I guess I generally look composed. . . . I've got nerves like anyone else, but in an emergency I don't let *them* take charge. The last thing I'll ever do is panic." It was this presence of mind under pressure, and the steady way he called pitches, that won him the respect of the Reds' pitching staff. It also earned him the nickname "The Little General," though at six foot one and 197 pounds, he could hardly be described as "little."

Bench was an excellent defensive catcher — some baseball experts think the best ever. His cat-quick reflexes let him pounce on bunts and snag pop flies and wild pitches. He blocked home plate with his body, even at the risk of injury. Even so, Bench proved to be remarkably durable, ranking fourth on the all-time list with 1738 games as catcher. Add to this an accurate, cannonlike arm, and it's easy to see why he earned the Golden Glove Award in each of his first ten years.

A look at his fielding stats bears out the praise. Bench is second on the list for chances by a catcher with 10,186, third in putouts with 9242, and eighth in fielding average at .991.

Bench's handling of pitchers and his fielding were so good he would have been the starting catcher on most teams even if he hit .200. But he was as determined while batting as he was while fielding. His third full year saw him have perhaps the best offensive season of any National League catcher. He had 45 homers and 35 doubles, knocked in 148 runs, and scored another 97, coming away with a .293 average. He would go on to hit 20 or more round-trippers eleven times, and leads all National League catchers in career homers. And his 1284 RBIs are also a career high for catchers.

More remarkable is the fact that he performed at a consistently high level despite injuries and other physical problems. The 1972 off-season had Bench operated on for a lesion on his lung. His shoulder was torn up when Gary Matthews of the San Francisco Giants dived into it while trying to score. That same year saw him hit in the ankle by a pitch. X rays showed that he'd had three previous breaks! Bench had played on all three while they were healing.

The injuries began to take their toll as early as 1976. He still put in time behind the plate, and his .533 average and two game-winning home runs helped earn him that year's World Series Most Valuable Player award. But his damaged body could take the day-to-day wear of catching less and less, and his playing time behind the plate was curtailed. Despite this, Bench managed to tie Bill Dickey's record of 13 seasons with 100 or more games catching.

There is little doubt that Bench was the heart of the powerful Cincinnati Reds team in the 1970s, providing not just a solid offense and defense, but a spirit that was unbeatable. And when he retired at the close of the 1983 season, many people considered him baseball's all-time catcher.

G	AB	H	2B	3B	HR	R	RBI	BB
2138	7648	2039	370	22	379	1072	1357	880

SO	SB	BA
1282	68	.267

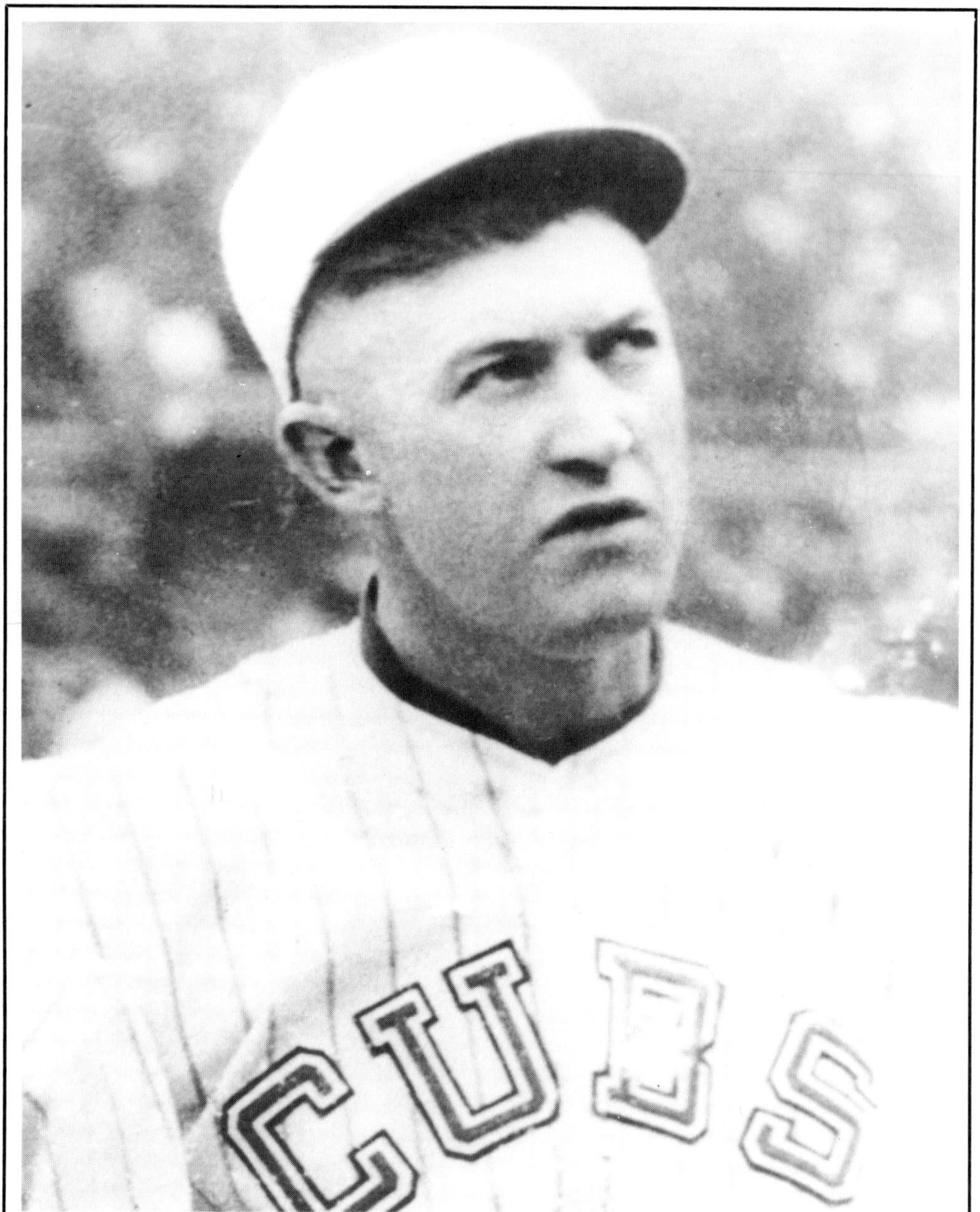
CUBS

☆ | PITCHER | ☆
GROVER CLEVELAND ALEXANDER

Grover Cleveland Alexander (Pete)
Born: February 26, 1887, Elba, Nebraska
Died: November 4, 1950, St. Paul, Nebraska
Career dates: 1911–1930   Hall of Fame: 1938
Batted and threw right-handed

It takes most major league pitchers a year or two to figure out the strengths and weaknesses of opposing hitters. But when Grover Cleveland Alexander (known simply as Pete to his teammates) joined the Philadelphia Phillies in 1911, he was a mature twenty-four years old with a wicked curve and fastball. He immediately dominated hitters, winning 28 games in his rookie year, including a league-leading 7 shutouts.

Curiously Alexander didn't come across as particularly impressive on the mound. He always looked as if he'd put his uniform on in the dark, and his cap never seemed to fit. Even his delivery was odd — a choppy, three-quarter windup that seemed careless. But despite his appearance and manner, Alexander got the job done.

Alexander went on mowing down hitters at a record pace for the next six years. In that span he won 165 games, while losing only 75, for a winning percentage of almost .700. He won 30 or more games three seasons in a row and led the league in shutouts four times. In 1916, he chalked up 16 shutouts, the highest single season total in major league history.

The startling thing about these totals is that he did it with a Philadelphia team that could best be described as erratic. They were weak hitters for the most part and suspect in the field. In fact, they only managed to attain respectable records on the strength of Alexander's arm.

Alexander's pitching pattern was relatively simple. He'd start batters off with curves, making them chase the ball if possible. Then, when he had two strikes on the batter, he'd fire a fastball by him for the called strike three. In his first eight years, Alexander led the league in strikeouts five times. In addition, he had uncanny control, walking only 953 batters during his twenty-year career.

It was almost as if Alexander, sensing his teammates would get him very few runs, did his best to shut out opponents. His lifetime of 90 shutouts is the second highest ever. And his earned run average of 1.22 in 1915 was a National League mark until Bob Gibson broke it in 1968.

Alexander might have sailed along like this for years except for World War I. While serving in the army, he lost his hearing in one ear because of the constant shelling. Shortly after this, he began displaying the symptoms of epilepsy.

Alexander returned to full-time pitching duty for the Chicago Cubs in 1919 and reestablished himself as the best hurler in the league, winning 16 games (9 of those shutouts) and having a 1.72 ERA. In 1920, he was 27–14, had a 1.91 ERA, and fanned 173 batters — all league-leading stats.

But 1920 would be the last superseason for Alexander. Upset over the frequency of his epileptic attacks, he desperately tried to hide them from teammates, sportswriters, and fans. Alexander began drinking heavily to ease the emotional strain he was under. His strikeout totals dropped, while batters began reaching him for more hits and runs. He remained an effective pitcher throughout the 1920s, twice winning over 20 games. And he never lost more games in a season than he won. Gone, however, was his ability to stop teams at will. Alexander retired in 1930, one of baseball's most haunting and misunderstood characters. His 373 wins is the third highest total all-time.

W	L	Pct	ERA	G	GS	CG	IP	H
373	208	.642	2.56	696	598	439	5189.1	4868

Relief Pitching

BB	SO	Sho	W	L	SV
953	2199	90	23	17	31

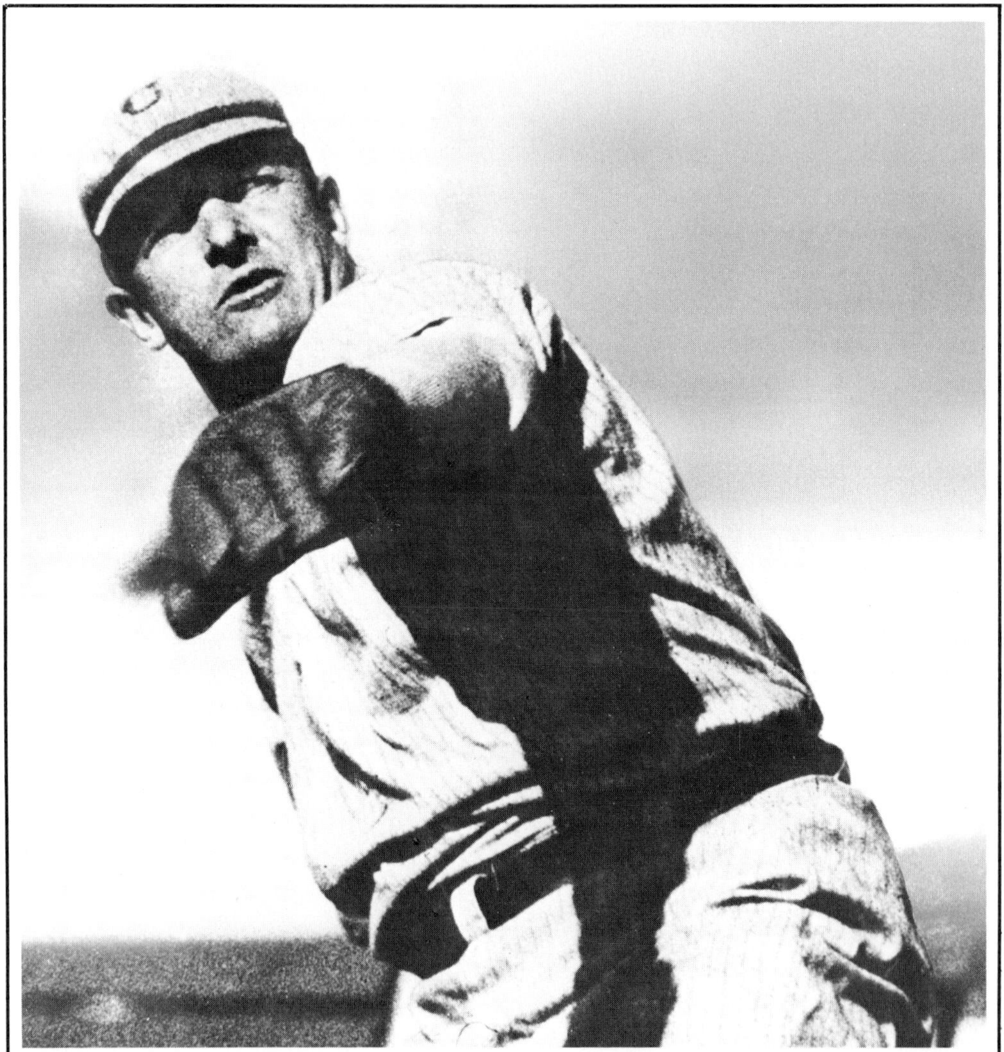

☆ | PITCHER | ☆
CHRISTY MATHEWSON

Christopher Mathewson (Big Six)
Born: August 12, 1880, Factoryville, Pennsylvania
Died: October 7, 1925, Saranac Lake, New York
Career dates: 1900–1916   Hall of Fame: 1936
Batted and threw right-handed

If baseball ever had a devil, it was the mean-spirited Ty Cobb. If it ever produced a saint, his name was Christy Mathewson.

During his seventeen years with the New York Giants, Mathewson was always a gentleman, soft-spoken and well mannered. He didn't drink and seldom smoked. And he was well educated, having graduated from Bucknell University. Add to this his striking good looks, and Mathewson is almost too good to be true.

His character alone would have set him apart from the other players of his era, who were generally poorly educated, hard-drinking, and hard-fighting men. But Mathewson also had something else going for him — he was one of the most skilled pitchers in baseball history.

His career wins are tied with Grover Alexander's for third best ever, while his winning percentage ranks sixth. His ERA is fifth best, and he's third in career shutouts. Mathewson even managed to be an excellent relief pitcher.

Mathewson's success rests on his mastery of two pitches: a wicked curve and the "fadeaway." He taught himself to throw a curve when he was eight years old by constantly hurling stones. His aim was so accurate he often hunted squirrels and birds with stones.

He picked up the "fadeaway" while in the New England League. The pitch was actually a reverse curve, breaking in on right-handers and away from lefties. Later, when the pitch was thrown by left-handed pitchers, it would be known as a screwball. Mathewson could place the ball so precisely that one player commented, "He could throw a ball into a tin cup at pitching range."

Evidence of his control can be found in his walk and strikeout totals. Mathewson gave up very few walks, averaging less than 1.5 per game (nineteenth lowest ever). During one month in 1913, he didn't give up a base on balls to anyone! In the strikeout department, he ranks sixteenth overall and led the league six times in this category.

The amazing thing about his strikeout totals is that he never tried to overpower batters. He realized that strikeout artists had to throw too many pitches in a game, risking fatigue and arm injury. He preferred to let batters hit into outs. His style of pitching meant he threw between 75 and 80 pitches a game instead of the usual 125, which accounts for his long and consistently successful career.

In seventeen years, he won 30 or more games three times, 20 or more thirteen times. During one incredible five-year stretch he allowed fewer than 2 earned runs a game.

Another part of his success comes from an intense study of opposing batters. Once he knew a hitter's strength, he rarely gave into it afterward.

If all this weren't enough, Mathewson was also a quick and agile fielder, a real plus in the days of high infield grass. He ranks third in total chances for a pitcher (1836), eleventh in putouts (281), and second in assists (1503).

Mathewson was traded to the Cincinnati Reds in 1916. He

pitched for them for a season and managed the team until 1918. Sadly, Mathewson, who'd led a charmed pitching life, died of tuberculosis just nine years later.

W	L	Pct	ERA	G	GS	CG	IP	H
373	188	.665	2.13	635	551	439	4783	4216

Relief Pitching

BB	SO	Sho	W	L	SV
846	2511	83	26	10	27

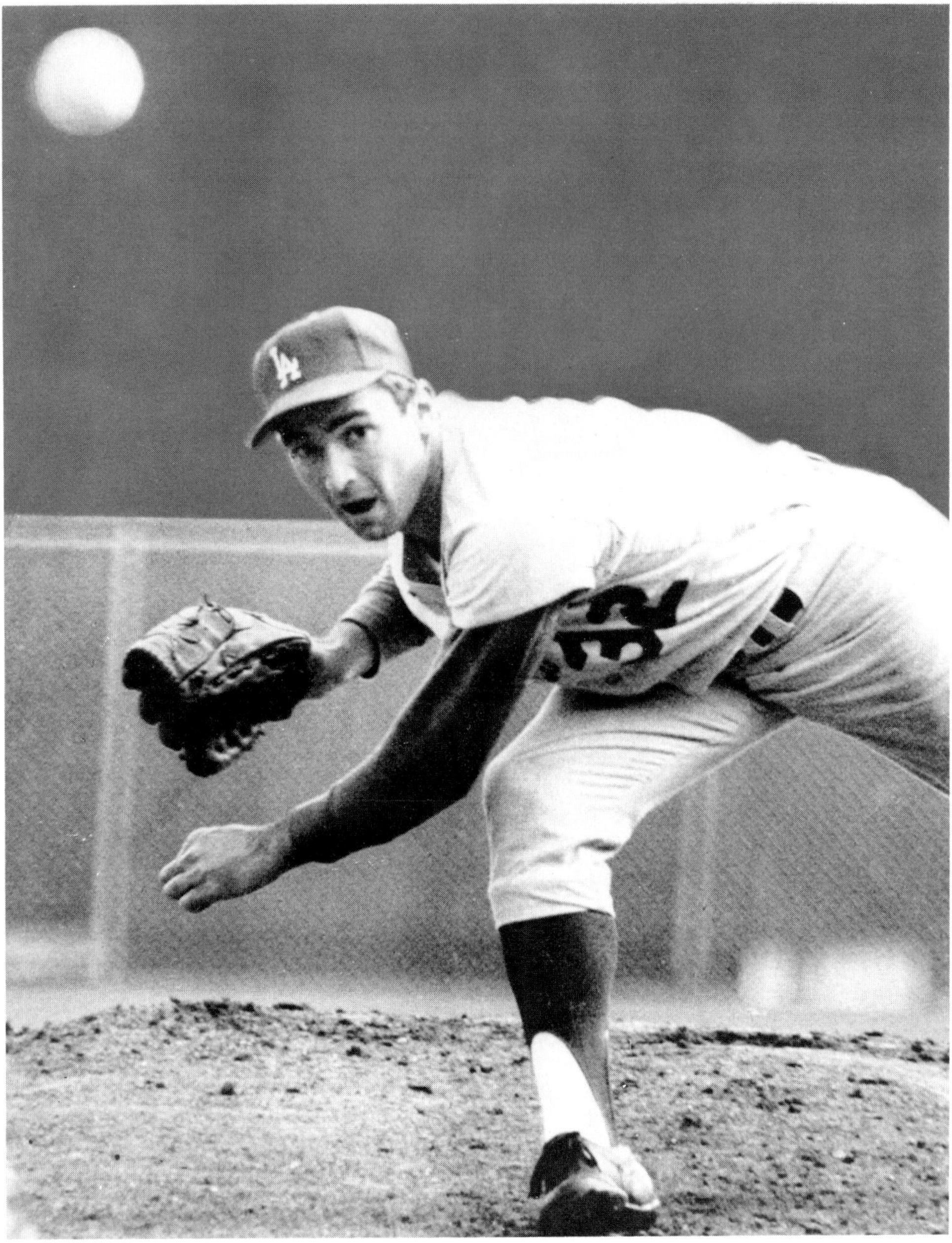

☆ | PITCHER | ☆
SANDY KOUFAX

Sanford Koufax
Born: December 30, 1935, Brooklyn, New York
Career dates: 1955–1966   Hall of Fame: 1971
Batted and threw left-handed

In a way, Sandy Koufax had two major league careers, each lasting six years.

The first covered the years 1955 to 1960. During that time, the six-foot-two, 210-pound southpaw had a blazing fastball but lacked control. In 1958, for instance, he had a league-leading 17 wild pitches.

Koufax's problem was one of self-confidence. If he threw a bad pitch and was tagged for a hit, he'd get down on himself. He'd begin rushing his pitches, trying to overpower the next batter with heat. Usually he ended up losing his pitching rhythm instead. He might have mastered this problem with some time in the minors, but his contract forbade his being sent down. So Koufax stayed on the Brooklyn Dodger staff and struggled to a mediocre 36–36 record for his first five years.

The year 1961 witnessed a profound change in Koufax's attitude. He was twenty-five that season, so maturity may have given him a stronger self-image and attitude. In addition, he had developed a change-up and a sharp curve to complement his fastball. His pitching was much more consistent that year, and while his record of 18–13 isn't overwhelming, he did chalk up a league-leading 269 strikeouts.

After this, Koufax was just about untouchable by hitters. In his second six years, he won a total of 129 games, while losing only 47 (and this with a team that gave him very little offensive support in the form of runs). During this time, he led the league in wins three times, ERA five times, strikeouts four times, and shutouts three times. His total of 382 strikeouts in 1965 is second only to Nolan Ryan's 383 as a single-season high, and his 11 shutouts in 1963 make him eighth best.

Probably the most astonishing thing is that of 40 shutouts, four were no-hitters. And one of these, pitched against Chicago in 1965, was a perfect game in which no batter ever reached first base (only ten have been thrown in the history of baseball).

But even as he was hurling a 27–9 record in 1966 with a 1.73 ERA, the end of his pitching days was in sight. He developed a rare circulatory problem that blocked 85 percent of the blood flow to his pitching arm. He lived with pain constantly that year as the skin on his left hand dried, then peeled. Koufax once described the raw flesh as feeling as if it were on fire, and his doctors warned him that he risked losing his arm if he continued pitching. Koufax wasn't even thirty when he retired, literally at the peak of one of the best six years of pitching ever seen in baseball history.

W	L	Pct	ERA	G	GS	CG	IP	H
165	87	.655	2.76	397	314	137	2324.1	1754

Relief Pitching

BB	SO	Sho	W	L	SV
817	2396	40	6	2	9

☆ | **PITCHER** | ☆

BOB GIBSON

Robert Gibson (Hoot)
Born: November 9, 1935, Omaha, Nebraska
Career dates: 1959–1975   Hall of Fame: 1981
Batted and threw right-handed

The word that best describes Bob Gibson's brand of baseball is *fierce*. He had a spinning, staggering pitching motion, with arms and legs flailing wildly. He didn't so much throw the ball as launch it. And if an occasional fastball rode in a bit tight on a batter, well, it served as a warning. The plate was Gibson's territory and not to be crowded.

He came up to the St. Louis Cardinals in 1959, though his first two years, posting a combined record of 6 wins and 11 losses, were ineffectual. He had a blazing fastball but, like Koufax, had difficulty maintaining control.

"Pitching is ninety percent thinking," Gibson would say about his early years. "I threw hard when I was younger, but I didn't know how to get people out."

After two years of "learning," Gibson became one of the dominant pitchers of his time (along with Sandy Koufax). He was able to place his pitches where he wanted them without having to hold back any or lose any of the ball's zip. His strikeout and shutout totals rose dramatically. He fanned 200 or more batters nine times, and his career shutouts are the tenth highest ever.

Gibson would go on to win 251 games in his career and have five seasons in which he won 20 or more games. His winning percentage is a solid .591, while his strikeout numbers rank sixth highest and his ERA is ninth best.

His numbers look even better when you remember that he pitched with a "lively" ball. Alexander and Mathewson pitched during the "dead ball" era, when the ball simply didn't come off the bat as quickly or travel as far.

Gibson aided his own cause by being a superb fielder, despite his spectacular pitching motion. He was extremely nimble around the mound, with the range of a fleet shortstop. Once he even rode down a ball that had bounded over his head and was heading up the middle for a hit. Gibson was so good out there that he won the Golden Glove Award from 1965 through 1973.

What made Gibson so good? What set him apart from other gifted pitchers? Most people would answer that it was his competitiveness. "The greatest competitor was Bob Gibson," Peter Rose has said. "He worked so fast out there . . . he always wanted to close his own deal. I sure as hell don't miss batting against him."

The intensity of this competitiveness knew no bounds either. During one game against Pittsburgh, Gibson took a lined shot by Roberto Clemente off his ankle. He went down in a heap but refused to come out of the game. He then pitched to three batters, getting two out, and running the count to the third to 3–2. During the payoff pitch, Gibson came down with his usual lunging follow-through and snapped the already cracked bone! He'd actually pitched to three batters with a broken ankle.

It was this fanatical drive that propelled him to one of the best seasons any modern-day pitcher has ever had. In 1968, he posted a 22–9 record for a .710 winning percentage. He struck out 268 batters, had 13 shutouts, and came away with an incredible 1.12 ERA. These are all league-leading numbers, with the ERA bettering the mark set by Grover Alexander.

Gibson's season was so outstanding that baseball authorities took notice, fearing that Gibson (and other hurlers) would reduce the number of home runs hit. In a curious backhanded compliment to Gibson's skill, they lowered the mound and made the strike zone smaller.

W	L	Pct	ERA	G	GS	CG	IP	H
251	174	.591	2.91	528	482	255	3884.2	3279

Relief Pitching

BB	SO	Sho	W	L	SV
1336	3117	56	6	4	6

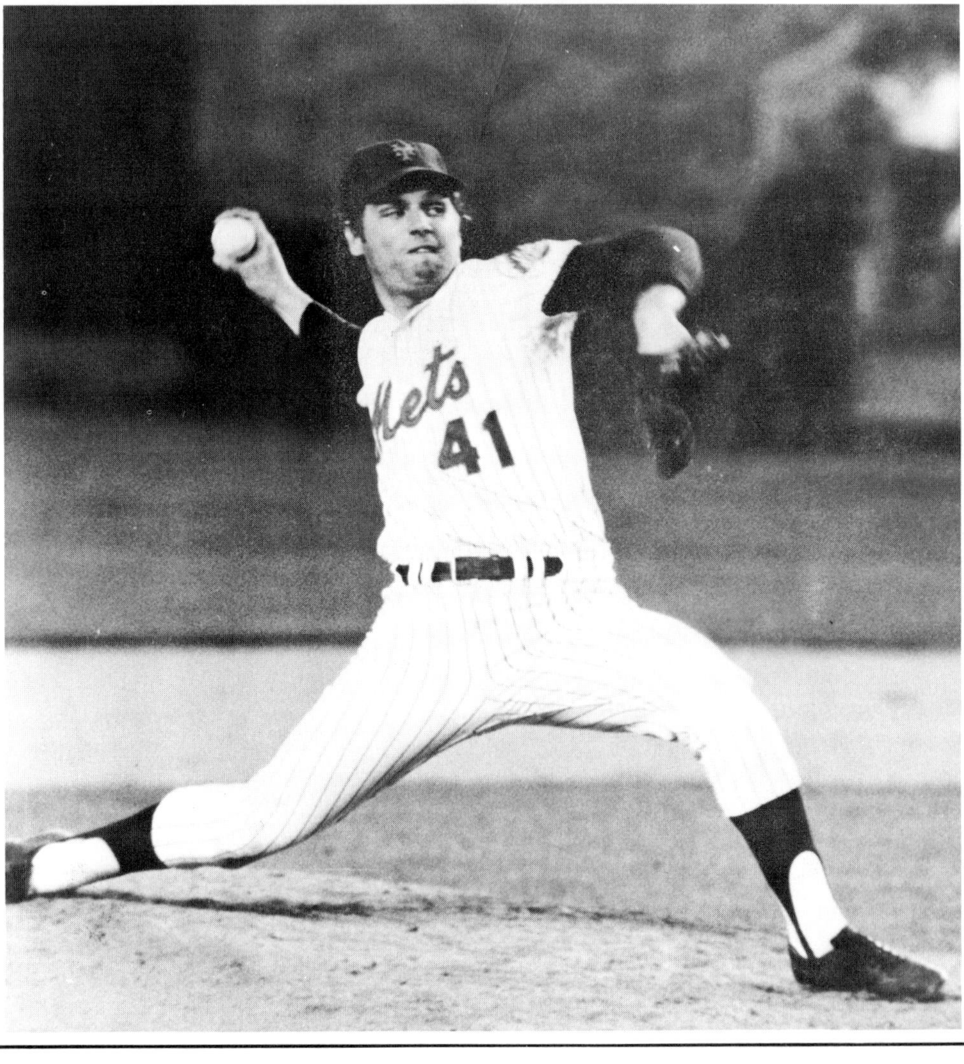
Mets
41

☆ | **PITCHER** | ☆

TOM SEAVER

George Thomas Seaver
Born: November 17, 1944, Fresno, California
Career dates: 1967–
Bats and throws right-handed

He was often referred to as "Tom Terrific," and no wonder. When he joined the bumbling Mets organization, he stood out like a new penny — poised and confident with a great slider and sinkerball.

Seaver spent only one season in the minors before being promoted to the parent club in 1967. During his first two years, the young right-hander had records of 16–13 and 16–12. But his won/lost log in no way reflects Seaver's true skill.

The Mets of that era were absolutely awful, providing little hitting or fielding support. They were "so pitiful that they were funny," one writer noted. Funny, that is, for everyone but a young pitcher who watched his best efforts fumbled away. The wonder is that Seaver won as many games as he did.

A truer indication of Seaver's ability can be seen in his strikeout, base on balls and ERA stats. He chalked up 170 and 205 strikeouts those first two years, giving up just over 50 walks a season. And his ERAs of 2.76 and 2.20 are remarkably low. Fortunately, the baseball community did recognize the magnitude of his achievement and voted Seaver Rookie of the Year for 1967.

The 1969 season showed what Seaver could do with just a

little support. The Mets were still a pretty mediocre team, but they managed to produce a few extra runs and improve their fielding. Seaver came out with a 25–7 record, a 2.21 ERA, and over 200 strikeouts as he led the Mets to their first pennant and World Series victory.

The fact that the team was dubbed the "Miracle Mets" was no accident. Whatever magic they possessed in 1969 evaporated in 1970 as they once again sank in the standings. Ironically, Seaver's career would be a roller coaster ride with teams that were hot one year, cold as ice the next. Even so, Seaver continued his effective control pitching, collecting twelve sub-3.00 ERA seasons. Most of these seasons took place after the mound was lowered and the strike zone reduced as a result of Bob Gibson's extraordinary 1968 season, making Seaver's stats even more impressive.

Along about 1970, Seaver added a blazing fastball, propelled in large part by incredible leg drive, that seemed to jump up just before reaching the plate. His strikeout totals rose, and he led the league five times in this category. His ten seasons with 200 or more strikeouts is a major league record. And he shares (with Philadelphia's Steve Carlton) the record for most strikeouts in a game (19).

The Mets would surge once more to win the 1973 pennant. Seaver went 19–10, with a league-leading 2.08 ERA and 251 strikeouts. The next year, they dropped again.

A contract dispute saw Seaver traded to the Cincinnati Reds midway into the 1977 season, and he ended the year with a 21–6 record and a 2.58 ERA. But while the Reds took a pennant in 1979, they were an aging team and subject to the same fluctuations as the Mets. And when Seaver rejoined New York in 1983, the Mets were a young team without much power or experience.

Through all of these ups and downs (and one run losses)

Seaver never lost heart, never lost the positive frame of mind a pitcher needs to be effective. He would win 20 or more games in a season five times, 15 games or more seven times.

Seaver stands twenty-eighth in career wins, fifteenth in winning percentage, sixth in strikeouts, and eighth in hits (giving up only 7.16 per nine innings). His career ERA average is the lowest of any pitcher in the lively ball era (since 1920). Not bad stats at all for a guy who had to do much of it on his own.

W	L	Pct	ERA	G	GS	CG	IP	H
273	170	.619	2.82	548	543	217	4090.0	3476

Relief Pitching

BB	SO	Sho	W	L	SV
1239	3330	56	0	2	1

THE AMERICAN LEAGUE TEAM

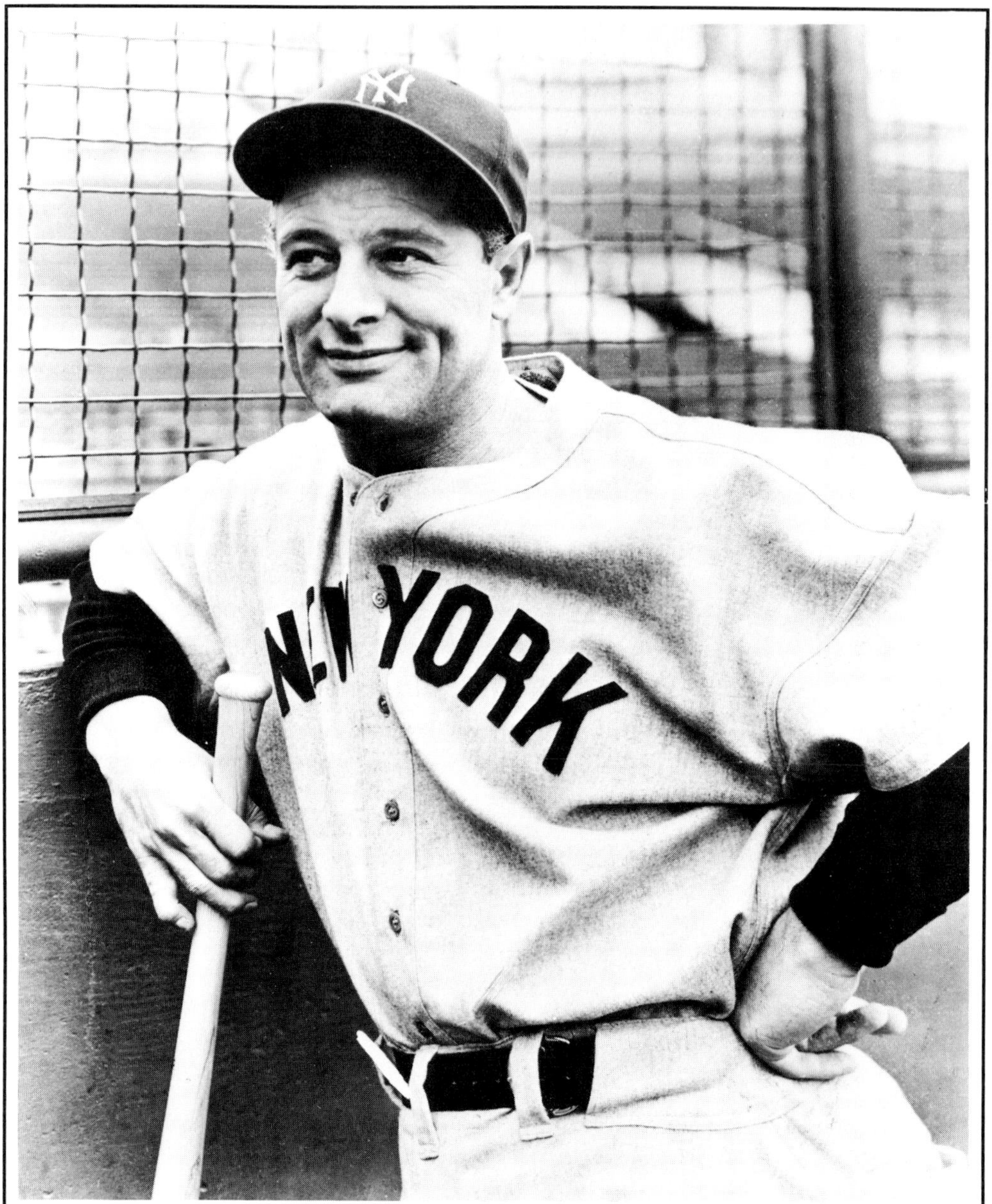
NEW YORK

☆ | **FIRST BASE** | ☆

LOU GEHRIG

Henry Louis Gehrig (The Iron Horse)
Born: June 19, 1903, New York, New York
Died: June 2, 1941, New York, New York
Career dates: 1923–1939   Hall of Fame: 1939
Batted and threw left-handed

When Lou Gehrig came to the Yankees in 1923, he was a bulky six-footer who didn't play baseball very well. He had been a sub-.200 hitter at the High School of Commerce in New York and a clumsy first baseman at best. He didn't even go out for baseball when he attended Columbia College. But New York Yankee scouts had been tipped off about Gehrig's awesome strength. In a special practice session he didn't hit the ball very often, but when he connected, he sent the ball screaming on a line shot to the wall.

Matching Gehrig's strength was his fanatical determination to make himself a better player. Even when he was a Yankee regular, he took extra fielding and batting practice. "No matter what his achievements," his wife Eleanor said, "he was dogged by a sense of failure and the need, constantly, to prove himself."

It was this determination that saw Gehrig through his first two seasons of sitting on the bench. While most players would have lost their enthusiasm for the game, Gehrig's seemed to grow. He watched his fellow teammates field their positions, and he asked Manager Miller Huggins hundreds of questions about baseball strategy. After each game, Huggins would hit grounder after grounder to Gehrig to help him improve his reflexes and fielding.

When Gehrig trotted out to first base to replace an injured Wally Pipp in 1925, he was ready for the big leagues. Exactly how ready would have shocked everyone. From that day on, Gehrig never missed a game until he retired fifteen years later. His 2130 consecutive-game streak is a record that will probably never be matched, and it earned him the nickname "The Iron Horse."

Gehrig's extra hours of practice made him a consistent, reliable player at first base. He learned to play behind the bag to give himself a split second longer to react to a ball hit in his direction. Although his fielding was never sparkling or inspired, he was the steadiest player in the game and always near the top in fielding average. And in thirty-four World Series games he fielded a near perfect .997.

But it was his bat that did the most talking for Gehrig. He would plant himself in the batter's box like a rock, his bat almost motionless, his eyes fixed on the pitcher. When he swung, his bat whipped around in a blur. He hit such hard line drives that most of his teammates referred to him as "The Buster."

The result was an incredibly steady hitting performance. He had eight 200-hit seasons and batted above .300 fourteen times, with six above .350! He led the league in home runs three times, runs four times, and RBIs five times. He even managed to amass 1508 walks, the tenth highest in baseball history.

But for all his ability, Gehrig never stirred up a lot of fan enthusiasm. In fact, many considered him a dull player, overshadowed by the flash of Babe Ruth and, later, the grace of Joe DiMaggio. Sportswriters considered him a "quiet plugger."

Gehrig longed for his share of fame, but it always eluded him. On the day he hit four home runs in four consecutive trips to the plate, he didn't even make the sports headlines. Ruth did — for overeating and having to be rushed to the hospital as a result.

If Gehrig was envious of others, he didn't show it, and it didn't affect his playing. His only comment about Ruth was a wistful "Babe sure knows how to live."

Then, after sixteen years, his career came to a sudden stop. During spring training and then during the regular season of 1939, Gehrig found himself constantly tired. He'd drop easy grounders or his legs would give way while running. He forced himself to play, but eventually he took himself out of a game and never returned.

Gehrig was diagnosed as having a degenerative disease that affects the motor pathways and cells of the central nervous system. The disease is called amyotrophic lateral sclerosis, though baseball fans know it as "Lou Gehrig's disease."

It's a shame that the image most fans have of Gehrig is that of a sickly man saying his farewell at Yankee Stadium. He was a giant of a player, possessed of enormous physical strength and enormous determination. Yankee manager Bucky Harris said it best: "When you consider everything, the number of games he played, the way he hit, his reliability and his drive, he was the greatest first baseman of all time."

G	AB	H	2B	3B	HR	R	RBI	BB
2164	8001	2721	535	162	493	1888	1990	1508

SO	SB	BA
789	102	.340

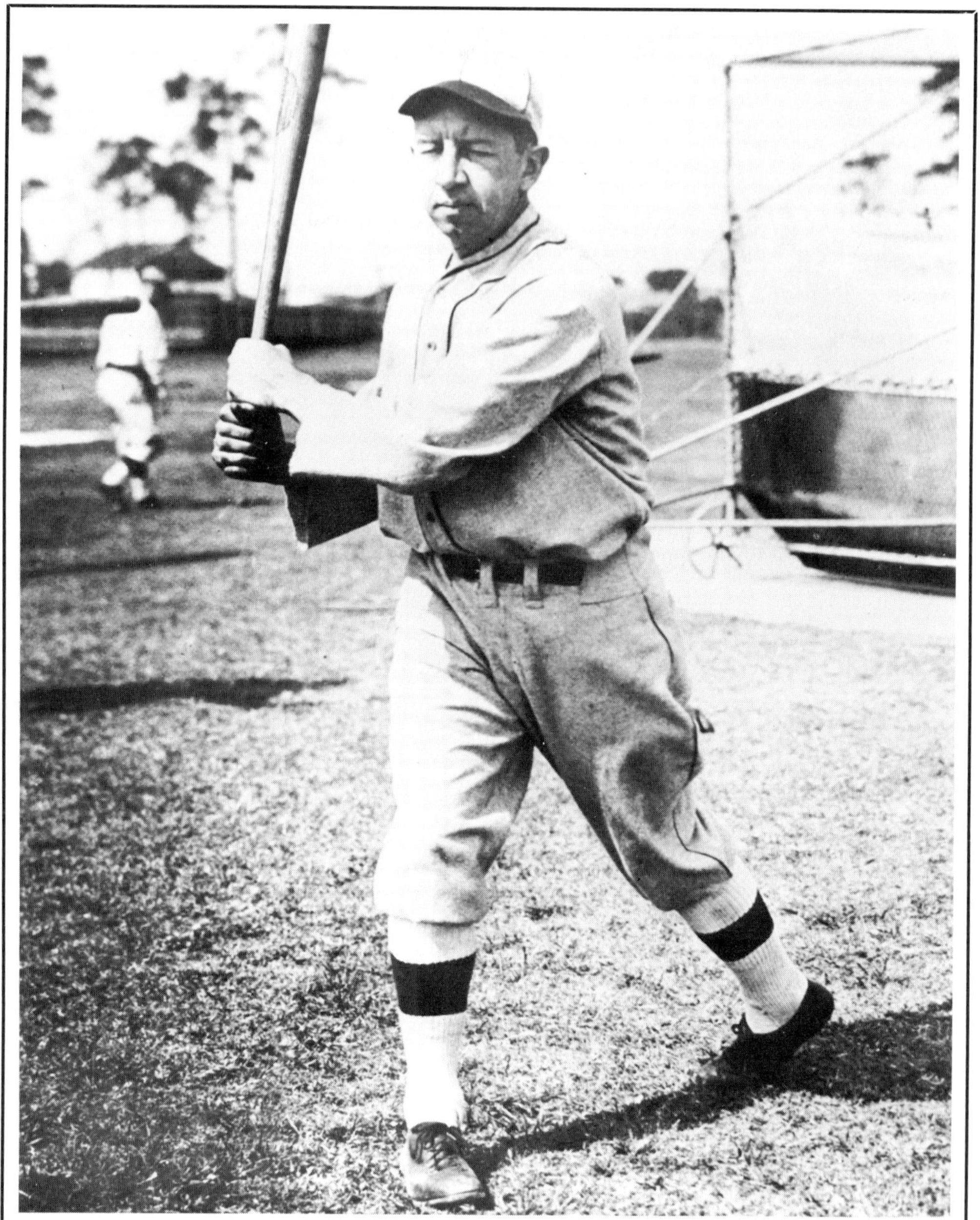

☆ | SECOND BASE | ☆
EDDIE COLLINS

Edward Trowbridge Collins
Born: May 2, 1887, Millerton, New York
Died: March 25, 1951, Boston, Massachusetts
Career dates: 1906–1930   Hall of Fame: 1939
Batted left-handed, threw right-handed

"It's something I'll always remember," Connie Mack, manager of the American League's Philadelphia Athletics team, would say of his first view of Eddie Collins. "He was fast, you could see that right off. And he never gave up on a ball. It was September 17, 1906, and I'll always remember it."

But if Mack had been impressed by the nineteen-year-old's raw talent, it wasn't enough to get Collins into the starting lineup right away. Mack had a policy of making young players sit on the bench for a couple of seasons, watching the veterans and learning baseball strategy. That's exactly what he had Collins do also. In 1906 and 1907, Collins got into a total of only 20 games. And in 1908, he played in 102 but was switched around from second base to shortstop to the outfield as he spelled other players. In 1909, however, he was made Philadelphia's starting second baseman, and he began to show his true ability.

Collins had breathtaking speed to his right and left and would chase grounders into the outfield if he thought he could make a play. "He was one of those determined types," a disgusted opponent would grumble after Collins had robbed him of a hit. This tremendous determination let him get his glove on a record number of balls. He holds the major league record in chances for a second baseman with 14,591. He also leads in putouts (6526) and assists (7630).

Collins was particularly graceful as the pivot man in double plays. He would take the ball while moving toward the bag, step on the base with his left foot for the force out, then leap high to avoid the incoming runner, while throwing to first for the second out. He ranks seventh in double plays at second with 1215.

His reflexes and speed allowed Collins to get involved in almost anything hit in his direction, but it was his consistency in the field that makes him great. He rarely bobbled the ball, despite using a glove no bigger than his hand. And he was always near the top in fielding average, leading the league nine times.

Collins was just as fast and consistent running the bases, too. His total steals rank third all-time, allowing him to lead the league in that department four times, once getting 81 thefts. Collins even managed to lead the league in steals in 1924, at the ripe old age of thirty-seven! And he ranks ninth in steals of home with 17.

His fielding and base running would have made any manager happy and kept him playing for many years. But with these Collins added a sharp (and consistent) batting eye. He would hit above .300 eighteen times, with a high of .369 in 1920. His base hit total is seventh highest in baseball history, while his career average puts him twenty-second on the list. And if further proof of his batting eye is needed, just look at his strikeout numbers — they average only a little over eleven a year!

Collins never hit many home runs, mainly because his career began in the dead ball era. He was schooled in making contact with the ball and not in aiming for the fences. Even so, he did collect a lot of extra base hits, getting 20 or more doubles thirteen times and 10 or more triples twelve times. This put him in position to score a lot of runs — which he did, winding up eleventh on the all-time list.

When the dough-faced Collins retired after twenty-five years in the majors, he'd played more games at second base (2650) than anyone else. And he had managed to hit, run and field superbly in just about every one of them.

G	AB	H	2B	3B	HR	R	RBI	SO
2826	9949	3311	437	187	47	1818	1503	286

SB	BA
743	.333

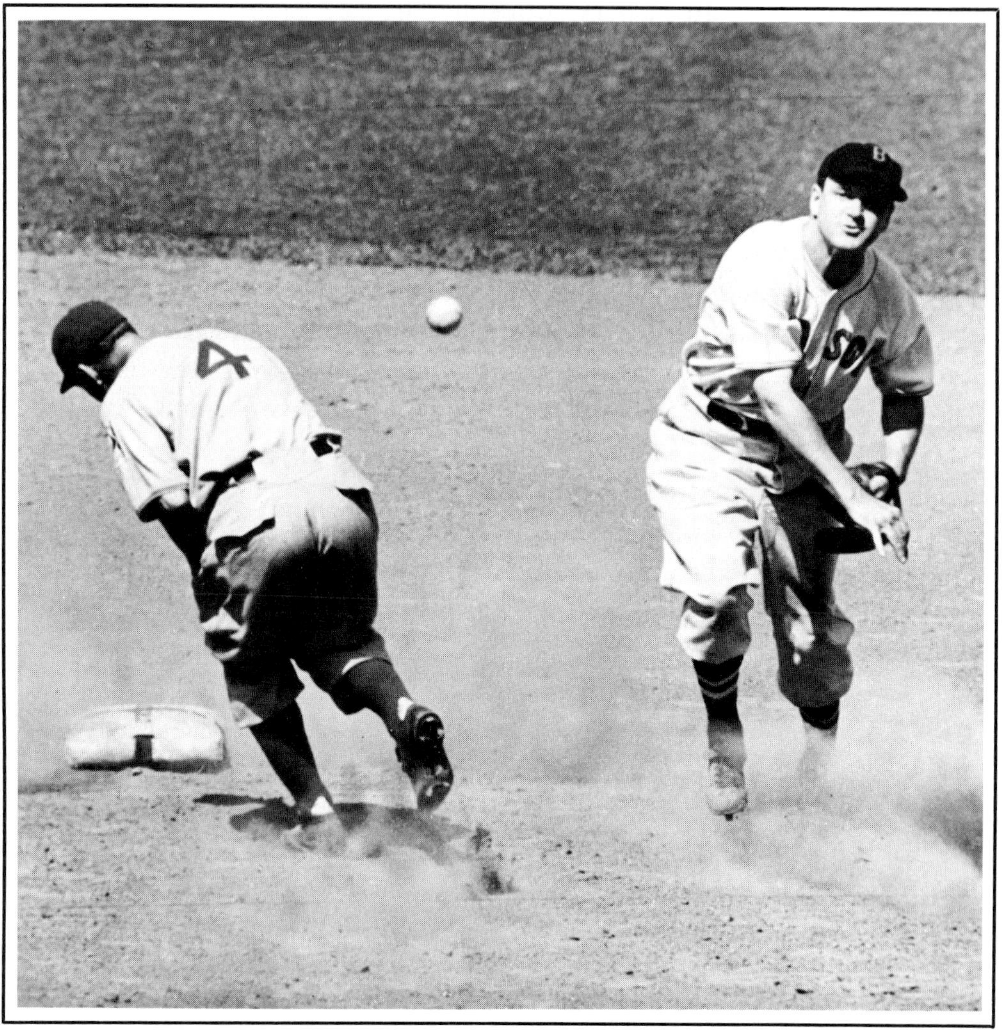

☆ | **SHORTSTOP** | ☆

JOE CRONIN

Joseph Edward Cronin
Born: October 12, 1906, San Francisco, California
Career dates: 1926–1945   Hall of Fame: 1956
Batted and threw right-handed

There are two out in the fourth, but the Boston Red Sox have men on second and third, and strong-hitting (at least in 1931 he was) Earl Webb at the plate. Webb slaps at the next pitch and sends it skittering along the dry infield grass toward the hole between second and third. A hit will score both runners easily.

The Washington Senators' pitcher, General Crowder, hardly has time to react before the ball is past him. Third baseman Ossie Bluege tries to short-hop the ball, but misjudges it and sees it skip over his glove.

The ball hits the edge of the outfield grass and takes a wild bounce into short left field. The next second, Washington's shortstop, Joe Cronin, makes a backhanded stab that snares the ball; he instantly wheels and fires a perfect strike to get Webb at first by a step. The inning is over, and Cronin's sparkling play has snuffed out a potential rally. It's the type of play Cronin made often, and it led to his being named Shortstop of the Year by the Baseball Writers Association in 1930, 1931, 1932, 1933, 1934, 1938, and 1939.

Curiously, Cronin's ability didn't come naturally. He had to work at it.

Cronin's first two years in the majors were with Pittsburgh, and for the most part they were spent on the bench. In his very first game, for instance, he threw one ball ten feet over the first baseman's head. Later in the same game, he booted an easy grounder. His play was so tentative that a teammate shouted out, "If you're going to miss 'em, Joe, miss 'em like a big-leaguer."

Cronin was traded to Washington in 1928. When he was made that team's full-time shortstop, his confidence began to grow. He seemed to relax in the field, and he began to allow his instincts and quick reflexes to dictate his moves. This, plus a thorough knowledge of opposing batters, let him anticipate where the ball might be hit. After 1929, he was always near the top in fielding average, leading the league in 1932 and 1933. And his participation in 1165 double plays ranks eleventh all-time for shortstops.

Most teams would have been perfectly happy with a strong fielding shortstop even if he couldn't hit very well. Certainly Cronin's first four years (when he hit .265, .222, .242, and .281) seemed to promise that kind of career for him. But Cronin wasn't satisfied. He began taking extra hitting practice with a team trainer, Socko McClary, learning to place his hits better.

During the winter of 1929–30, Cronin also decided to build up his muscles. Every morning he'd run four or five miles into the Black Hills of Dakota. Then he'd chop wood for the rest of the day. When he returned to spring training in 1930, he was a hefty 180 pounds with strong arm and back muscles.

That year, Cronin's hitting leaped into high gear. He batted .346, including 203 hits, 41 doubles, and 126 RBIs. He would go on to hit above .300 eleven times after this, regularly collecting 100 or more runs and RBIs.

Cronin was named manager of Washington in 1933 and led his team into the World Series with a .309 average and a league-leading 45 doubles. He was traded to Boston in 1935 and became player/manager for eleven years. Remarkably, Cronin's playing didn't suffer despite his managerial duties and the resulting pressures. His fielding actually seemed to improve, while his hitting remained consistent and run-producing.

Eventually, however, the physical strain of playing shortstop and a series of nagging injuries began to take their toll on Cronin. He saw limited playing time in 1941, preferring to let younger players take over at his position. Despite reduced action, Cronin still managed to produce key hits. He went 18 for 42 as a pinch hitter in 1943 (for a .429 average, eighth highest for a single season), including 5 home runs.

As in all sports, luck plays a part in baseball. But if Joe Cronin had left his game to luck, he might have been an erratic fielder and a modest hitter — qualities that usually earn a player a quick trip home. Cronin took his natural abilities and molded them, coming away as one of baseball's rarest phenomenons, a great fielding *and* hitting shortstop.

G	AB	H	2B	3B	HR	R	RBI	BB
2124	7579	2285	515	118	170	1233	1059	1059

SO	SB	BA
700	87	.301

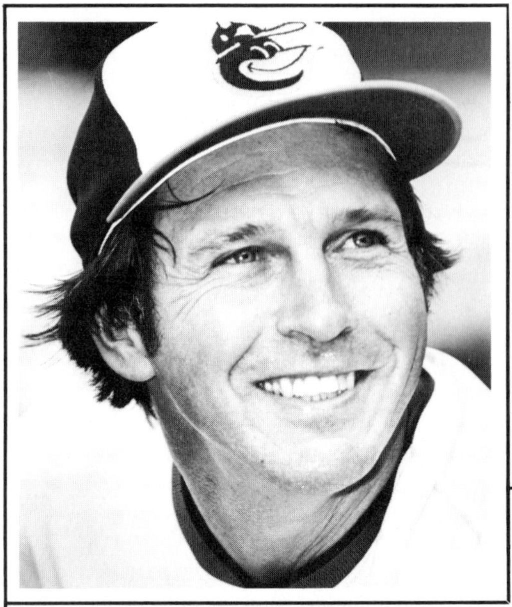

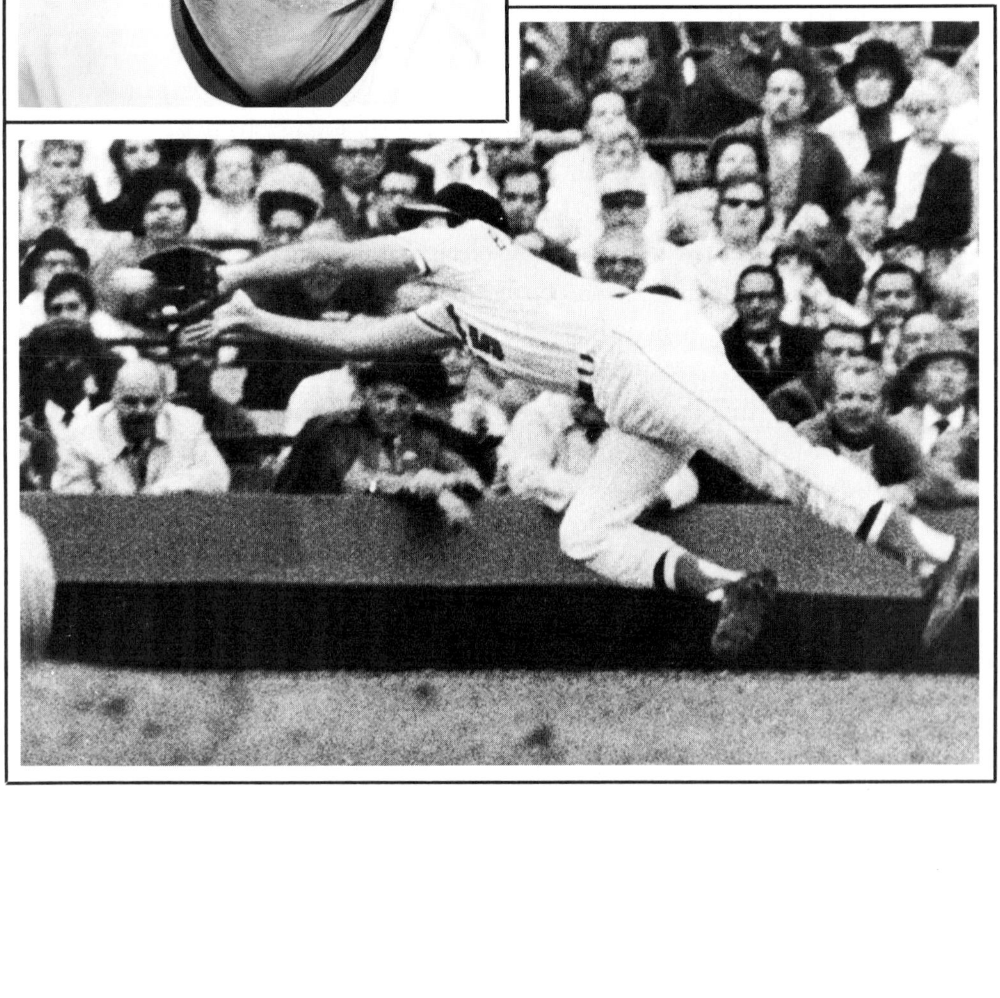

☆ | THIRD BASE | ☆
BROOKS ROBINSON

Brooks Calbert Robinson
Born: May 18, 1937, Little Rock, Arkansas
Career dates: 1955–1977   Hall of Fame: 1983
Batted and threw right-handed

As the pitcher delivers the ball, third-baseman Brooks Robinson poises expectantly, his eyes riveted to the hitter. He knows the pitch will be an inside fastball just below the knees. He also knows the batter is a pull hitter. The ball tails in on the batter, and Robinson plants his left foot in front of his body and leans toward the bag.

The crack of the bat sounds like a rifle shot, loud and solid. The ball blasts up the line, an indistinct waist-high blur heading toward the outfield at 120 miles per hour. But even before the batter has a chance to leave the box, Robinson has launched his body toward the line, his arms fully extended, his glove reaching. The ball thwunks into Robinson's glove, and the play is over. Another out. Another great play by Robinson.

The wonder of Brooks Robinson wasn't that he made catches such as this. It was that he made them routinely, day in and day out for his entire twenty-three-year career with the Baltimore Orioles. The twisting leap across third base, and the bare-handed stab at a dying bunt followed by an off-balance throw to first, were his trademark. And they earned him sixteen straight Golden Glove Awards as the league's best fielder at his position.

Robinson's lifetime fielding stats are worth repeating. He is first in chances at third (9165), first in putouts (2697), first in assists (6205), and first in double plays (618). If the ball headed his way, Robinson almost always managed to glove it. When he retired in 1977, he had the all-time high fielding average for the position, .971.

"I once thought of giving him some tips," said National League great Pie Traynor, "but I dropped the idea. Robinson is wonderful on every type of play. He's just the best there is."

What made Robinson the best was a combination of physical and mental qualities. He had exceptionally sharp reflexes—some say the best of anyone who played third. And while he wasn't noted for his running speed, his lateral movement was startling. Above all was Robinson's aggressive fielding attitude. Off the field he was a quiet, modest, and likable guy. But if the ball entered his area of play, it was a physical challenge that had to be collared, knocked down, stopped dead before it escaped into the outfield.

In all of the fuss over his fielding, Robinson's hitting is often overlooked. Granted, he always ran hot and cold at the plate, falling into some horrendous slumps. Yet his .267 career average is more than respectable, especially considering the beating his body took in the field. His 2848 hits put him twenty-eighth on the all-time list, and his runs and RBI totals are both in the top 100.

In the end, however, Brooks Robinson will always be associated with his dazzling glovework. The 1970 Cincinnati Reds team remembers it vividly. Just in the third game alone, Robinson crushed three Cinci rallies. In the first inning he snagged a chopping grounder to start a double play; in the second he robbed Tommy Helms of an infield hit; later in the game he speared a Johnny Bench liner just inches off the grass. Of Robinson's performance in the Series, Pete Rose said, "Brooks Robinson belongs in a higher league."

G	AB	H	2B	3B	HR	R	RBI	BB
2896	10654	2848	482	68	268	1233	1357	860

SO	SB	BA
989	28	.267

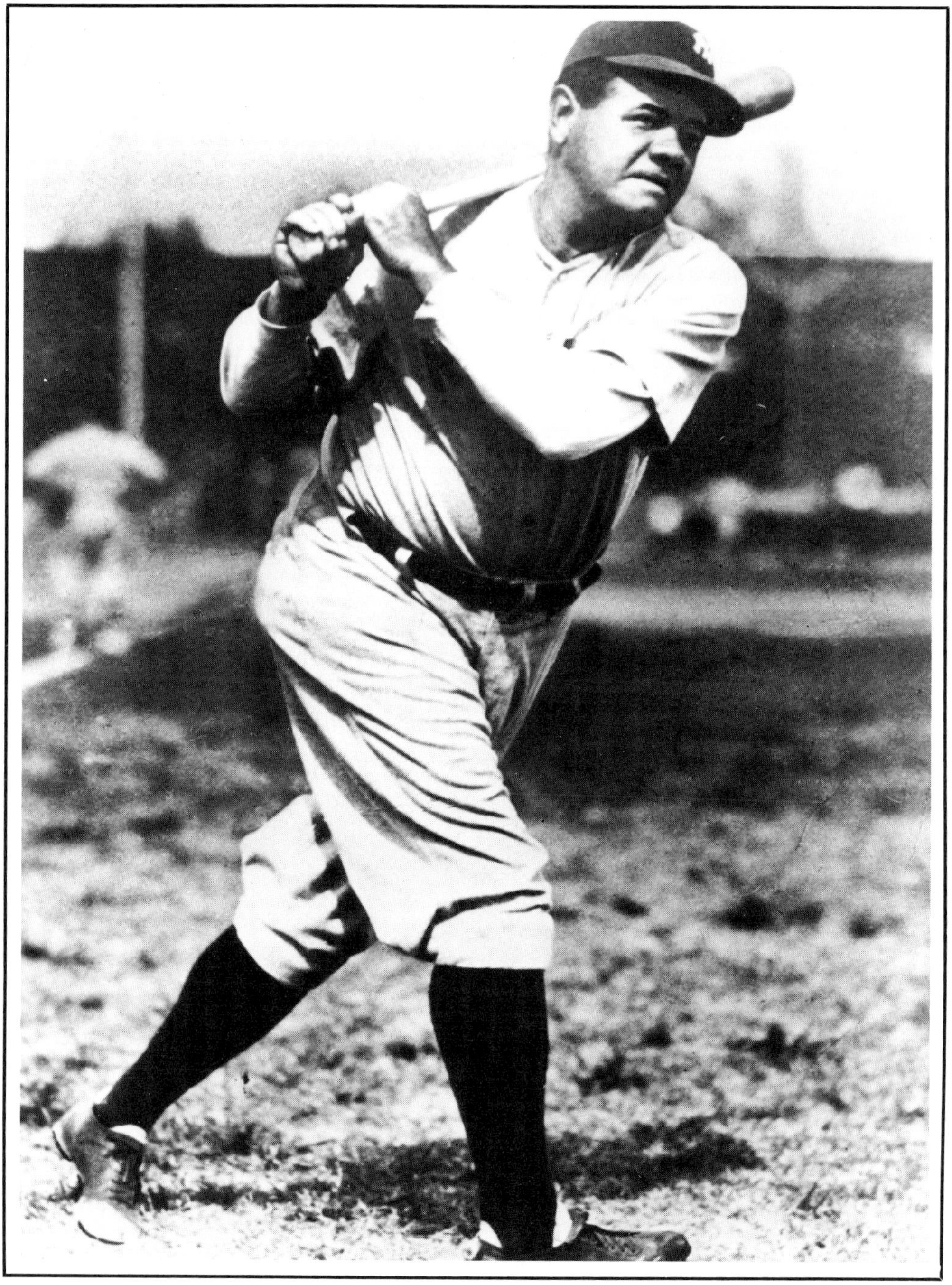

☆ | RIGHT FIELD | ☆
BABE RUTH

George Herman Ruth (The Sultan of Swat)
Born: February 6, 1895, Baltimore, Maryland
Died: August 16, 1948, New York, New York
Career dates: 1914–1935   Hall of Fame: 1936
Batted and threw left-handed

Mention the name Babe Ruth and most fans think of prodigious home runs and a wild life-style. Both responses are true to a degree. But the legend of Ruth has become so fixed that it often overshadows an accurate view of the man and his real skill as a ball player.

George Herman Ruth was born in Baltimore in 1895. When he was seven his parents divorced, and he was placed in St. Mary's Industrial School. He would remain a ward of the state of Maryland for fourteen years. While at St. Mary's he bumbled his way through classes, learned to be a tailor, and pitched for the school team.

His strong arm attracted the attention of a local minor league team's owner, Jack Dunn, who signed the nineteen-year-old Ruth as a pitcher. But in order to do this, Ruth had to be released to the care of Dunn. Teammates immediately began referring to him as "Dunn's baby," which later became shortened to "Babe." A few months later, Dunn sold Ruth's contract to the Boston Red Sox.

Ruth proved to be anything but a babe on the mound. He had a blazing fastball that overpowered batters. Ruth's career pitching marks are excellent. He won 94 games, including 17 shutouts, while losing only 46 times for a .671 winning percentage. His control was sharp, as seen in his 2.28 earned run average. Ruth won all three World Series games he pitched in, posting the third lowest ERA of 0.87. He even set a Series mark of 29⅔ consecutive scoreless innings, a record he held until eclipsed by Whitey Ford in 1961.

But as great a pitcher as he was, Ruth's hitting was already attracting a surprising amount of attention. In 1915, for instance, he hit .315 with 4 homers. His home run number might not sound very impressive in light of today's totals, but baseball was much different back then. The ball was "dead" and simply didn't carry very well. Teams built runs with walks, steals, singles — and not homers. Ruth's 4 home runs were only three short of Chicago outfielder Braggo Roth's league-leading 7!

After several such solid hitting performances, Boston wanted Ruth's bat in the lineup more often. In 1918 he played 59 games in the outfield and 13 at first (along with pitching in 20 games). The decision to play Ruth at other positions had to be one of the best in baseball history. Ruth batted .300 and hit 26 doubles, 11 triples, and a league-leading 11 four-baggers.

Ruth's 1918 season marked the beginning of an era of power hitting that stretched for sixteen years and earned him another nickname: The Sultan of Swat. It was also a time when his life-style caught the attention of the press. At age twenty-one he became legally independent and made the most of it, eating at the best restaurants, drinking lots of beer, and driving fast. His reaction to freedom after fourteen years of being a ward of the state is understandable. He was just a kid, after all, who also happened to be an ace on a World Champion team.

Fortunately for Ruth's career, Boston manager Bill Carrigan was able to keep his young phenom in line, at least enough to concentrate on playing ball while on the field.

Later, Ed Barrou would take over as Ruth's mentor at Boston and New York.

Ruth played 130 games at left field in 1919, hitting .322 and leading the majors in home runs (29), runs (103), and RBIs (112). His pitching was sharply curtailed, though he managed a 9–5 record. Following this remarkable year, Boston traded Ruth to the Yankees. Why trade an established superstar? Boston needed money and couldn't resist the then-astronomical $125,000 purchase price for Ruth's contract. The Yankees moved Ruth to right field — and Ruth went on hitting.

A glance at Ruth's stats shows that he not only continued his mighty hitting, but actually got better. Over his career, Ruth led the league in home runs twelve times, collecting 40 or more eleven times. He drove in 100 or more RBIs thirteen times, and scored 100 or more runs twelve times. His lifetime totals in these three categories are second best on the all-time list. Imagine what they might have been if his first five years were spent in full-time hitting!

In the midst of all this power, Ruth's real hitting skill is often overlooked. He batted above .370 six times, with a high of .393. His career average ranks eleventh all-time. He collected a surprising number of doubles (just 17 fewer than the fleet Willie Mays, though Ruth played 489 fewer games). His sharp batting eye, as well as pitchers trying not to give him anything good to hit, resulted in 2056 walks, the highest total ever.

Despite storklike legs and weight that ballooned to 215 pounds, Ruth had surprising speed. He combined this with his knowledge of opposing batter's hitting patterns to get a jump on balls hit to right and made some spectacular catches. No one would compare Ruth's fielding to that of Mays, for example. But Ruth was steady in the field with a more than respectable fielding average.

As his hitting onslaught carried one Yankee team after another to the pennant, Ruth became a media figure who rivaled — and surpassed — any modern-day Reggie Jackson. He was adored by fans. And everything he did made it into print, whether it was flipping his car while joy riding, attending all-night parties, eating twenty-five hot dogs, or blasting yet another game-winning home run. On the day Lou Gehrig hit four consecutive homers, a feat accomplished only three times in baseball history, it was Ruth who captured the headlines. He'd eaten too much and been rushed to the hospital.

The Yankees were even evicted from the Polo Grounds because of Ruth. The Yankees shared playing time there with the Giants, but when Ruth and the Yankees began to consistently outdraw the Giants by huge numbers, Charles Stoneham, owner of the Giants *and* the Polo Grounds, threw them out! That's why Yankee Stadium is often referred to as "The House that Ruth Built."

But behind the headlines there was another Ruth. His lifestyle calmed considerably after he married his second wife, Claire Hodgson. He was devoted to his family and friends, always warm-hearted and generous. He treated fans well, too, unlike some stars who turn their backs on the fans as bothers. And Ruth was genuinely fond of children, visiting hundreds of them in hospitals and shelters.

In 1930, just as the nation's worst depression settled in, Ruth hit the peak of his earnings with an $80,000 salary. When a reporter commented that he was making more than the president, Ruth answered, "I had a better year." But these were the days of hard-nosed and powerful management, and Ruth's salary was cut to $75,000 in 1932, despite a .341 average and 41 home runs. He was cut again a year later to $52,000, even while hitting .301 and 34 homers. He grew unhappy in New York, as well he should have, and was traded to the Boston Braves in the National League. He played only 28 games in 1935.

Many people grumble at the change Ruth's bat brought to baseball, feeling the home run has taken much of the skill out of the game. That may be true of modern players, but it's not Ruth's fault. Ruth was an accomplished all-around player, hitting for average and power, collecting walks, and fielding his position admirably. The home runs, however, are what he will always be remembered for. When asked why he tried to hit so many, Ruth's only comment was, "Because the people wanted to see me hit home runs and I got a kick out of hitting them."

Ruth retired when he was forty-one years old, overweight, and tired of the way management had treated him. On the Sunday before his last game, Ruth came to bat four times. He got a single and three titanic home runs. The last homer — number 714 — flew over the right-field grandstands of Chicago's Forbes Field, the only time anyone has ever hit a ball out of that park.

Lifetime Pitching Totals

W	L	Pct	ERA	G	GS	CG	IP	H
94	46	.671	2.28	163	147	107	1221.1	974

Relief Pitching

BB	SO	Sho	W	L	SV
441	488	17	2	2	4

Lifetime Batting Totals

G	AB	H	2B	3B	HR	R	RBI	BB
2503	8399	2873	506	136	714	2174	2204	2056

SO	SB	BA
1330	123	.342

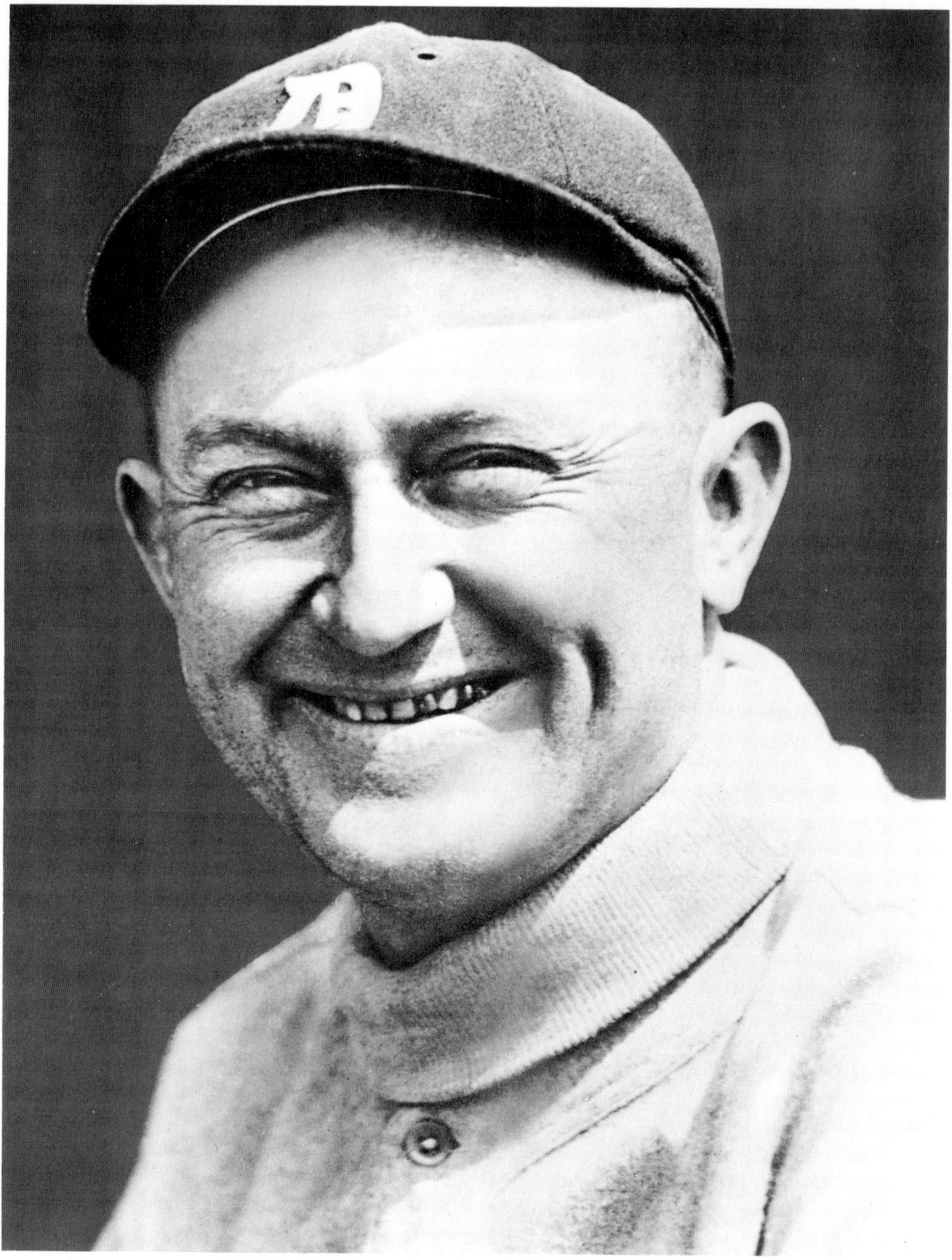

☆ | CENTER FIELD | ☆

TY COBB

Tyrus Raymond Cobb (The Georgia Peach)
Born: December 18, 1886, Narrows, Georgia
Died: July 17, 1961, Atlanta, Georgia
Career dates: 1905–1928   Hall of Fame: 1936
Batted left-handed; threw right-handed

Ty Cobb was the most hated man to have ever been in baseball. He was also one of the greatest players of all time.

When Cobb first appeared in a Detroit Tiger uniform, he was a mean-eyed, six-foot-one-inch-tall eighteen-year-old who held his bat like a club. That day he managed to slap out a double to left center, the first of his record 4191 hits.

But Cobb found himself an outcast from the start. Most of his Tiger teammates were northerners and unused to his Georgia twang. What's more, they openly ridiculed his rough-and-tumble style of play.

"The hazing I took from those men made me mad," Cobb recalled years later. "I found out the manners my family taught me had no place in baseball. I decided to forget being a gentleman and be tougher and meaner than any of them."

And he was! Cobb went into each game as if it were combat. He was fierce, unpredictable, and daring. "I always went into a bag, full speed and feet first. I had on sharp spikes, too. If the baseman stood there and got hurt, it was his fault."

Cobb made fun of opposing players to upset them and their game. He goaded, argued with, and often fought his own teammates to make them play better. He was so despised that a few of his own teammates even tipped off opposing pitchers to what they thought were Cobb's weaknesses.

But if he had a weakness, no one ever found it.

His speed was legendary. It allowed him to roam center field and make diving catches that others wouldn't have gotten close to. It helped him chalk up 892 stolen bases in his twenty-four-year career, and to lead the league in steals six times. He also holds the record for steals of home with 35. More than just speed, he ran as if he owned the base paths. It wasn't uncommon to see Cobb score from second base on a sacrifice bunt. And on at least four occasions he managed to get a single and then go on to steal second, third, and home! A few catchers didn't even bother to try to toss out Cobb. Instead, they'd throw a base ahead of the one he was stealing to hold the damage down.

Along with his speed and fielding he had a talent for hitting that has never been matched. He studied pitchers carefully, noting the kinds of pitches they'd use in different situations. This knowledge, plus an awkward-looking hands-apart grip that gave him near-perfect bat control, allowed him to pull or push the ball wherever he wanted it to go. His hitting stats include nine 200-hit seasons, a staggering number of doubles and triples, and a record number of runs scored, 2244. He led the league in hitting twelve times and had 23 consecutive seasons where he hit over .320.

Each year seemed to bring Cobb greater success and more fame. It also brought him more enemies. He lived apart from his teammates and never allowed any of them to get really close to him. His bickering with fans resulted in his once being stabbed while out for a drive. He even argued with his children and his wife. A teammate once summed up Cobb's personality: ". . . a few of us who really knew him well realized he was wrong in the head — unbalanced. He played like a demon and had everybody hating him because he *was* a demon."

When Cobb retired from the game in 1928, he had amassed some amazing records — and almost no friends. After his wife divorced him, Cobb spent his remaining years going from one cheap hotel to another, talking — and arguing — baseball with anyone who would listen. He died in 1961, a lonely, bitter man of seventy-five. Only three people from baseball bothered to attend his funeral.

G	AB	H	2B	3B	HR	R	RBI	BB
3033	11429	4191	724	297	118	2244	1959	1249

SO	SB	BA
357	892	.367

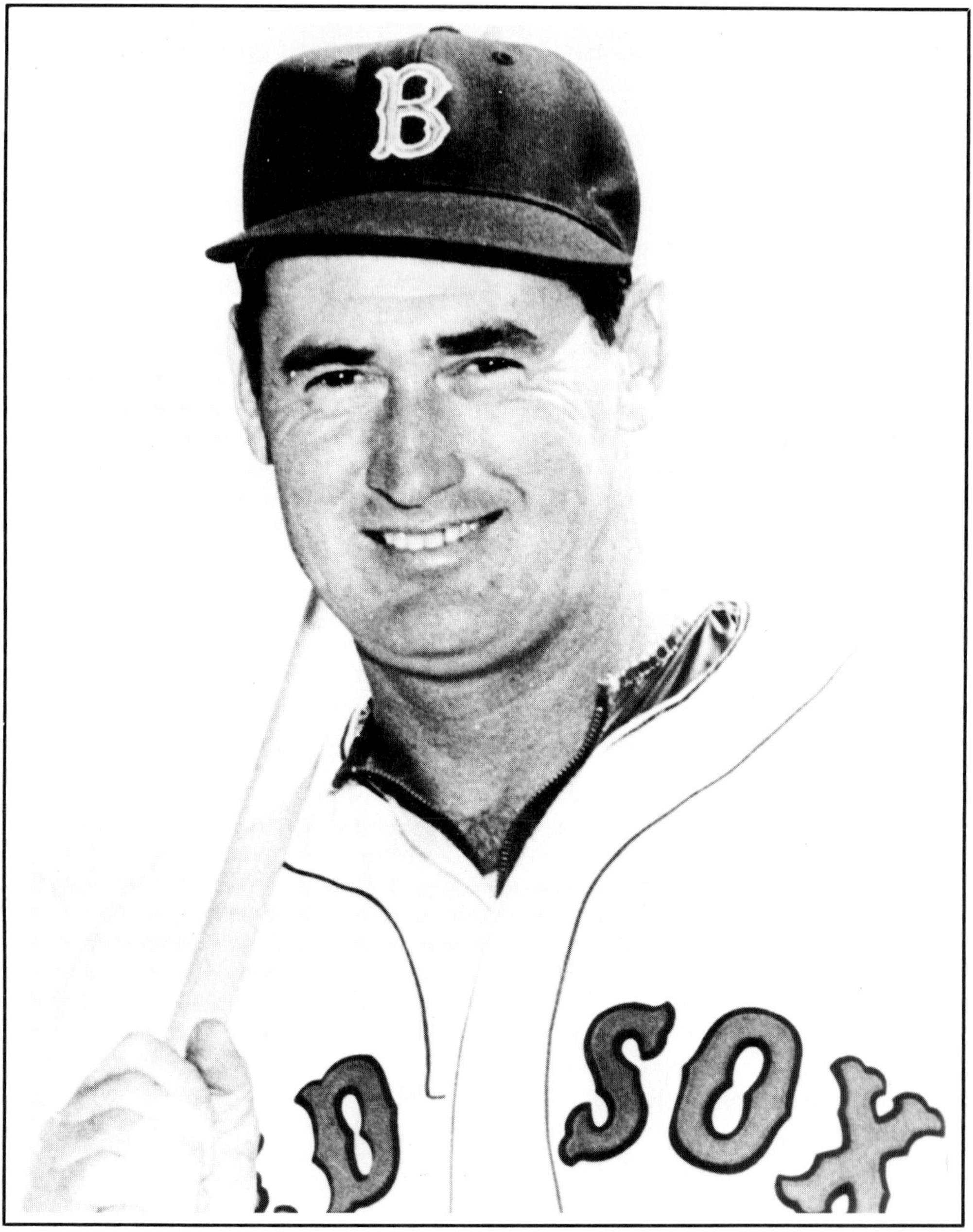
SOX

☆ | LEFT FIELD | ☆
TED WILLIAMS

Theodore Samuel Williams (The Splendid Splinter)
Born: August 30, 1918, San Diego, California
Career dates: 1939–1960   Hall of Fame: 1966
Batted left-handed; threw right-handed.

Ted Williams refined the art of hitting to a precise science. He was also baseball's bad boy, spending much of his time feuding with sportswriters, snubbing fans, or sulking.

Theodore (Ted) Williams was born and raised in San Diego. His parents divorced when he was young, and he often had to fend for himself. This might account for his stubborn independence, occasional moodiness, and the fierce way he defended his privacy. In fact, not much is really known about his childhood. But one thing certain about his early years is that from the time he was eleven he practiced his hitting whenever he could.

When he came up to the Boston Red Sox in 1939 at age twenty-one, Williams was a skinny six-foot-three inches tall (a fact that earned him the nickname "The Splendid Splinter"). While most players, even the greats, take a couple of years to adjust to major league pitching, Williams's rookie year is among the best in baseball history. He had 185 hits for a .327 average. More impressive, he banged out 31 homers and 44 doubles and had a league-leading 145 RBIs.

But Williams wasn't satisfied with this performance. He

immediately dedicated himself to improving his hitting, spending hours in the batting cage trying to perfect his swing.

Williams's first step was to discipline himself not to swing at bad pitches. He established a well-defined strike zone and forced himself to lay off balls that were out of the strike zone by even an inch. To avoid overswinging, he adapted a wide stance. His goal was to make solid contact with the ball and not try to overpower it. After his second season, the number of times he struck out dropped, while his walks went up dramatically. He would lead the league in walks eight times and wind up second all-time in this category.

Aiding Williams in his hitting were his almost superhuman eyesight and strong wrists. These allowed him to follow the ball's flight carefully and wait to the last possible moment to swing. Finally, Williams studied pitchers, figuring what mannerisms or small movements they might make when throwing a particular pitch.

Williams dominated the league in hitting during his next seven seasons. He averaged well over 30 doubles a year and led the league in homers four times, totaling 234 in this period alone. And he collected over 100 runs and RBIs each season, taking these titles six and three times, respectively.

Most power hitters, especially those after 1940, tend to sacrifice average for home runs. They upper-cut at the ball in hopes of parking it in the seats. Adding to a hitter's problems are the bigger fielder's gloves, artificial turf, which helps the ball get to the fielders quicker with few wild bounces, and relief pitchers. But Williams defied the odds and hit for power and average, leading the league in batting six times. He captured two triple crowns (for most homers, RBIs, and highest average), something achieved by only one other player in baseball history, Rogers Hornsby. And in 1941, Williams hit .406, the last player to go over .400.

Williams was injured in 1950 and several times thereafter. His playing time was curtailed slightly, as was his power. His home run and RBI totals slipped (though they still make most modern players' stats seem weak in comparison). But while his power stats declined, his hitting eye never wavered. Only once in his career would Williams hit below .300, and that was the direct result of an injury. He even won batting titles when he was thirty-nine and forty, hitting .388 and .328, and ended with the sixth highest average all-time.

As with most outstanding hitters, Williams's fielding is pushed to the background, possibly because it simply wasn't as brilliant as his hitting. He was tentative in his rookie year, committing a league-leading 19 errors in right field. But after being switched to left, he worked on his fielding with the same dedication he used in his hitting, reducing his errors in succeeding years. Twice he would commit only one error in an entire season, and his fielding average climbed until he was always near the top.

The curious element in the midst of Williams's exceptional play was his less than admirable personality. The Boston fans loved him, but Williams steadfastly refused to acknowledge them, saying their cheers would turn to boos as soon as he struck out. Odder still was his attitude toward the press, an attitude that could sometimes go to extremes. Once, when a writer from *Sport* magazine interviewed his mother, Williams became so angry at the intrusion that he refused to speak to anyone from that publication for twelve years. And when he crossed the plate after hitting home run number 500, he spat in the direction of the press box to show the writers exactly how he felt about them.

Why the hostile attitude? It's possible he was simply moody, going through periods when he needed to be alone but found himself constantly the focus of press attention. It's also possible that at times the fanfare interfered with his ability to concentrate on his hitting. And, of course, the press does have a tendency to overreact, to downplay the positive qualities of a person in order to create a story. The truth is that Williams did have many positive aspects. He would often seek out a newspaperman to give him a story, and he was deeply involved in raising funds for Children's Cancer Hospital in Boston.

When Williams retired in 1960, he had some impressive stats — second all-time in walks, eighth in home runs, and ninth in RBIs. They take on even more weight when you realize that Williams missed almost five full seasons in the prime of his career, first from 1943 to 1945, when he served in World War II, then again in 1952–1953 for the Korean War. If he had played these five seasons at the same level as those before and after, he would have hit over 700 home runs and 3000 hits and probably would have been the all-time leader in runs and RBIs. But what he left behind is pretty spectacular as is.

G	AB	H	2B	3B	HR	R	RBI	BB
2292	7706	2654	525	71	521	1798	1839	2019

SO	SB	BA
709	24	.344

☆ | CATCHER | ☆
BILL DICKEY

William Malcolm Dickey
Born: June 6, 1907, Bastrop, Louisiana
Career dates: 1928–1946   Hall of Fame: 1954
Batted left-handed; threw right-handed.

When Bill Dickey came up to the New York Yankees in 1928, he was a lean six foot one and was noted for his defensive skills and rifle arm. But while the Yankees had high hopes for Dickey, his hitting was suspect. In fact, in a series of stints with minor league clubs, he never came close to hitting .300.

Yankee manager Miller Huggins began working with his young catcher immediately. He advised Dickey to choke up on the bat and to forget about always going for home runs. Huggins was so confident in Dickey's ability to learn that he predicted he was "destined to be one of the greatest catchers in the game."

Dickey spent most of his rookie season on the sidelines, practicing his hitting before and after games, asking teammates for tips, and studying opposing pitchers for weaknesses. He became the starting catcher for the Yankees in 1929 and produced an impressive .324 batting average. Dickey would go on pounding the ball, hitting above .300 in ten of the next eleven years, with a high of .362 in 1936.

In addition to solid hitting, Dickey was one of the greatest fielding catchers in the history of the game. His exceptionally quick reflexes let him knock down and smother errant pitches other catchers might have missed. And while he wasn't very fast on the base paths, he could bound after foul pops or bunts with startling speed. What's more, he had an accurate and strong arm whose throws cut down runners effortlessly.

Even more important was the way Dickey called pitches. Studying opposing batters with the same dedication he'd used to learn to hit, Dickey memorized their strengths and weaknesses. Once familiar with a batter's habits at the plate, he rarely called the wrong pitch. "He's something more than a great hitter," said Cincinnati pitcher Paul Derringer after a Series loss to the Yankees. "He's a great thinker, and mechanically he's just about perfect."

Dickey's performance is even more impressive when you consider the physical beating a catcher takes. He had to call for and catch over a hundred pitches a game while wearing heavy equipment and crouching in the hot sun. Add to this the wild pitches he had to block, foul tips that smashed his fingers, and collisions with runners barreling into home. Throughout his eighteen years in the game, Dickey had his share of injuries, too. He broke the thumb and each finger in his throwing hand at least once. His kidney was injured in a collision at home, and he tore ligaments in his right arm. But through it all, Dickey managed to play. He even caught the 1936 World Series with a broken wrist. His durability is proved by his catching 100 or more games in 13 straight seasons, a record unmatched until Johnny Bench equaled it in 1980.

Injuries began to catch up with Dickey in 1940, and his hitting tailed off slightly during his last five years. But even as his playing career was gradually ending, another job with the Yankees began. He took on the task of training his successor as catcher, Yogi Berra, teaching him defensive tech-

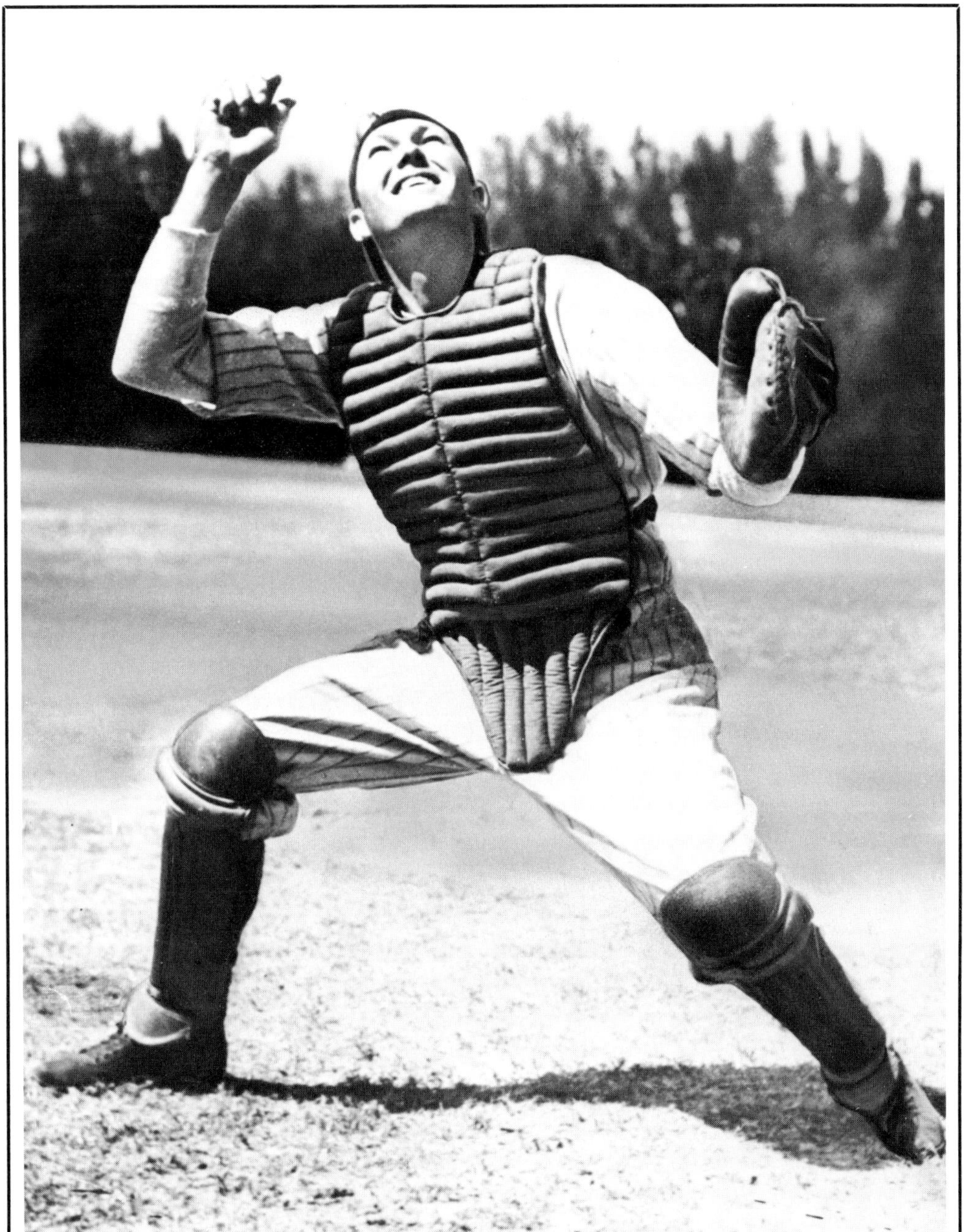

niques such as how to field bunts, throw out runners, and call pitches. Dickey's ability to communicate helped Berra become one of baseball's best fielding catchers. Later, Dickey would repeat the process with another great Yankee catcher, Elston Howard. Of Dickey's help, Howard said: "You know, that No. 33 is a genius. Nobody teaches baseball better than he does."

Through seventeen seasons Dickey called plays and fielded at a consistently excellent level despite a series of painful injuries. This alone would have ranked him as a great catcher. But when you add to this a solid hitting ability and the rare talent of being able to teach others the art of catching, you have a player who more than fulfills Huggins's prophecy: Bill Dickey was one of the greatest catchers in the game.

G	AB	H	2B	3B	HR	R	RBI	BB
1789	6300	1969	343	72	202	930	1209	678

SO	SB	BA
289	36	.313

☆ | PITCHER | ☆
EDDIE PLANK

Edward Stewart Plank (Gettysburg Eddie)
Born: August 31, 1875, Gettysburg, Pennsylvania
Died: February 24, 1926, Gettysburg, Pennsylvania
Career dates: 1901–1917   Hall of Fame: 1946
Batted and threw left-handed

When talk gets around to baseball's greatest pitchers, the names most mentioned are Walter Johnson, Mathewson, Koufax, Gibson, and a handful of others. Eddie Plank's name rarely comes up during these discussions. This is partly because his Philadelphia Athletics team usually finished well down in the standings (and therefore got little newspaper coverage outside of Philadelphia). In addition, Plank never amassed a lot of individual pitching records.

For instance, when Philadelphia finished a surprising second in 1903, Plank had a 23–16 record with a 2.38 ERA. But it was first place Boston's Cy Young who took the headlines with a 28–10 record and a 2.08 ERA. The next year, Plank and Young both registered 26 wins, but it was Jack Chesbro's 41 victories that led the league. And so it was, year after year — Plank was always close to, but never at, the top of the pitching categories.

If Plank ever became disappointed or irritated by these near misses, he never let it show. He was a quiet, poker-faced man who would rather work on his pitching than his public image. The result was one of baseball's most consistently successful pitching careers ever. After his second season, Plank rattled off 15 straight sub-3.00 ERAs, something no other pitcher has ever done. He registered 100 or more strikeouts thirteen years in a row, a record he shares with Detroit's Mickey Lolich. And he notched 20 or more victories eight times, coming away with the ninth highest career total.

Plank accomplished this with a good fastball and a sharp curve, both thrown with pinpoint accuracy. "He was very studious out there," said Boston's Smokey Joe Wood. "He used to pitch to spots. They didn't do that much in those days. But Eddie Plank did it."

And he did it well. He gave up very few base on balls, averaging only 62 a season. And his 70 shutouts rank fifth on the all-time list.

Plank was even consistent in his fielding. He could scoot off the mound in either direction so well that he helped throw out 1108 hitters, fifteenth best.

In a way, Plank was to pitching what Hank Aaron was to home runs. Neither actually dominated in the yearly stats, but their longevity and consistency let them accumulate outstanding career stats. So the next time anyone wonders about baseball's greatest pitchers, mention the name Eddie Plank. You might get some questioning looks, but like a Plank pitch, you'll be right on the money.

W	L	Pct	ERA	G	GS	CG	IP	H
327	192	.630	2.34	622	528	412	4513.1	3956

Relief Pitching

BB	SO	Sho	W	L	SV
1072	2261	70	23	14	25

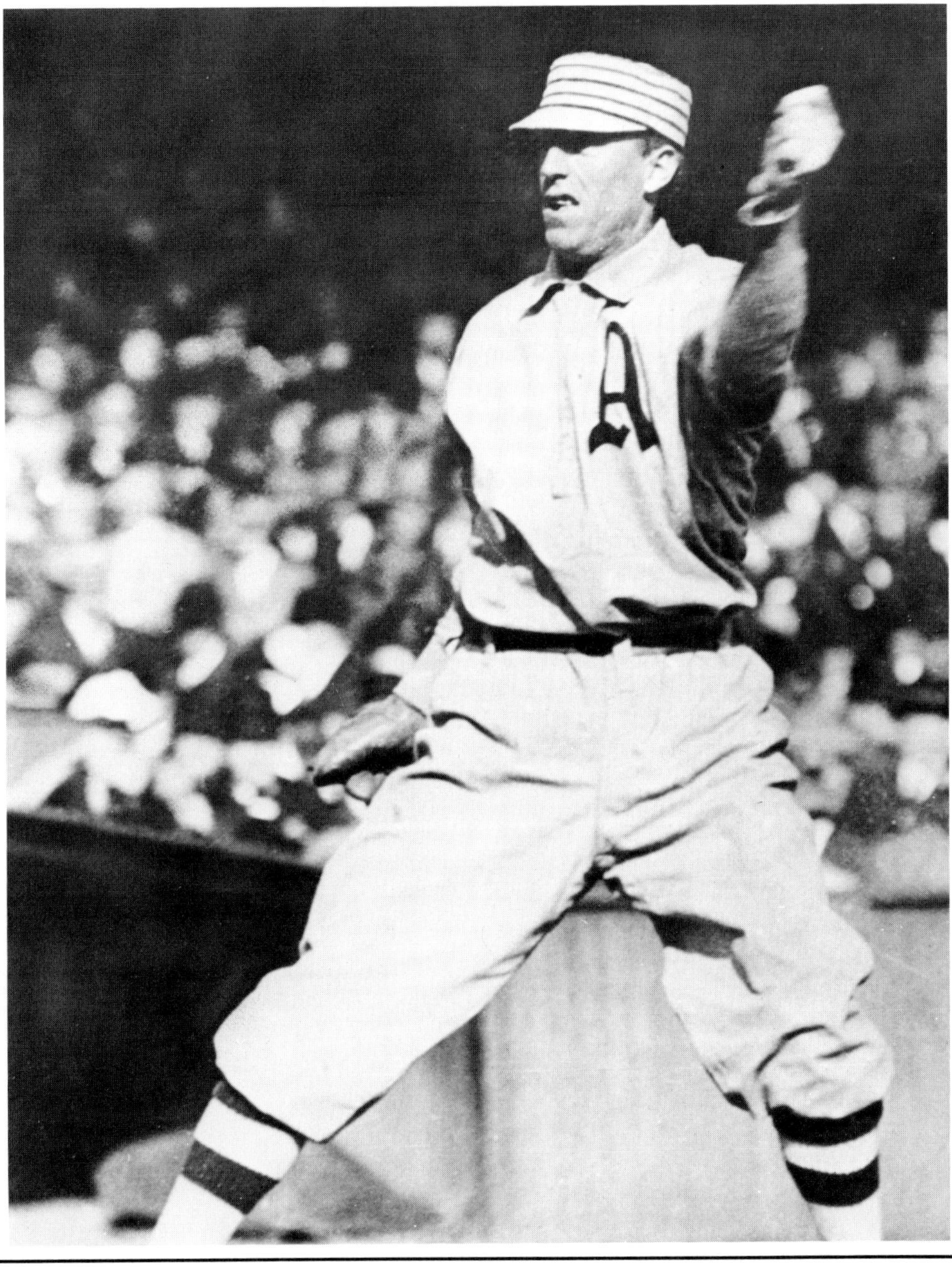

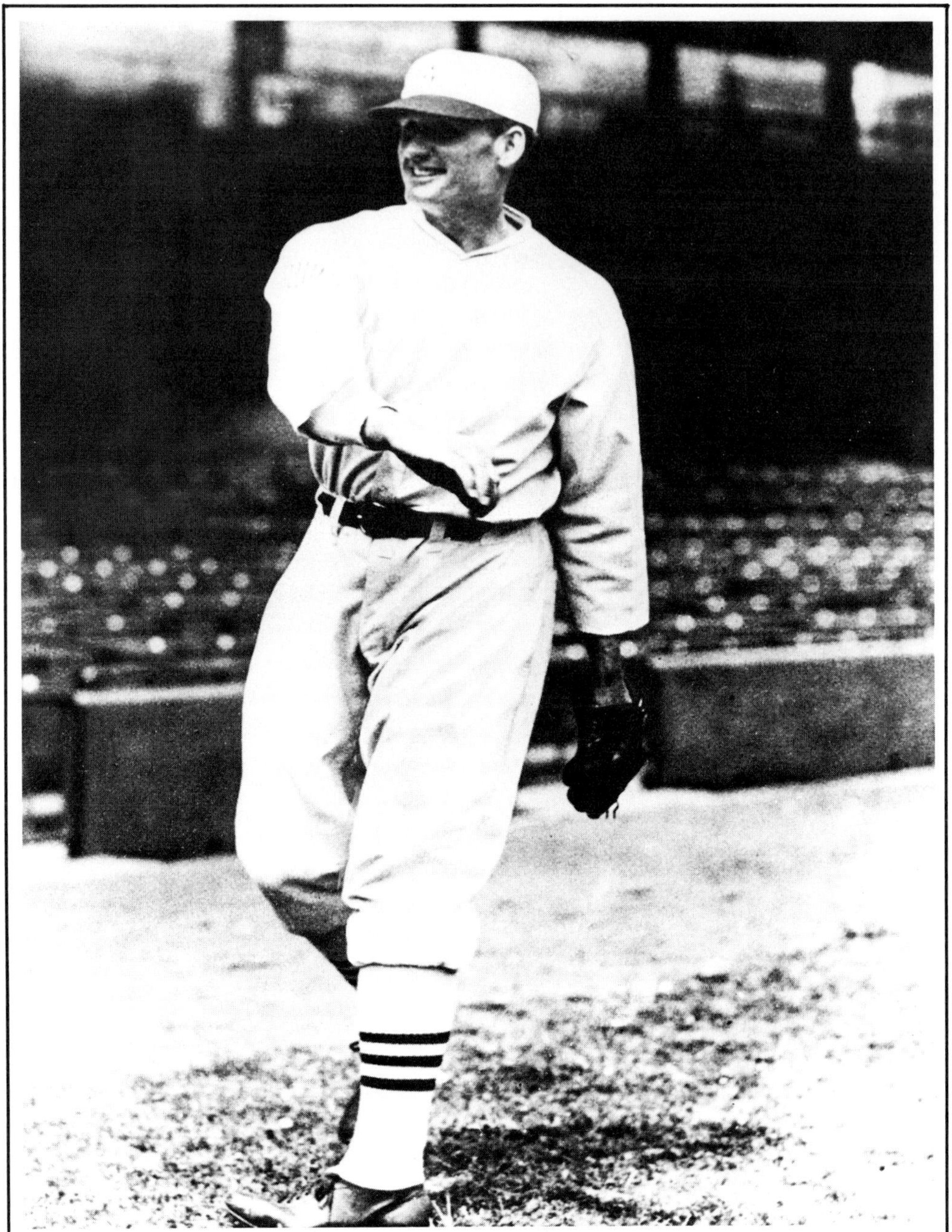

☆ | PITCHER | ☆
WALTER JOHNSON

Walter Perry Johnson (The Big Train)
Born: November 6, 1887, Humboldt, Kansas
Died: December 10, 1946, Washington, D.C.
Career dates: 1907–1927   Hall of Fame: 1936
Batted and threw right-handed

Ty Cobb said of his first-time batting against Walter Johnson, "On August 2, 1907, I encountered the most threatening sight I ever saw on a ball field. He was a tall, shambling galoot of about twenty with arms so long they hung far out of his sleeves and with a side-arm delivery that looked unimpressive at first."

Then Cobb stepped into the batter's box and watched the rookie right-hander take an easy windup — and something hissed by menacingly for a called strike. That was Johnson's style of delivery: a windup that appeared as if he were just playing catch and a fastball that came in like an express, a fact that earned him the nickname "The Big Train."

Johnson was a hulking kid when he came up to the Washington Senators, six foot one and 200 pounds. Yet despite his size, he was shy and gentle. What's more, he had a fear of hurting an opposing batter with his fastball that amounted to a phobia. He never threw at a batter on purpose, even though it was a common practice back then. This concern about hitting a batter may have made Johnson master control of his throwing early on in his career. Jon Cantillon, his manager in 1907, said, "He knows where he is throwing the ball because if he didn't there'd be dead bodies strewn all over Idaho."

Walter Johnson had the speed and control from the very beginning, but his won/lost record for his first three years doesn't show this. He went 5–9 in 1907, followed by 14–14 and 13–25 records. He was a rookie, of course, and unused to the knowledgeable hitters of the time such as Cobb, Wahoo Sam Crawford, and Frank (Home Run) Baker. He was also a so-so fielder at the start, particularly bad at handling bunts. In fact, after Cobb's initial shock at Johnson's speed, he laid down a perfect bunt for a single, and scooted all the way to third when Crawford followed Cobb's bunt with one of his own and the young pitcher booted it. The biggest factor in his won-lost record was his team. Washington was simply miserable, probably as bad as the Met team Tom Seaver found himself a part of.

A better indication of Johnson's pitching comes from his ERA averages, which were 1.87, 1.64, and 2.21 during those first three seasons. Then there was the time he beat the Yankees three times in four days in 1908, winning 3–0 on four hits on Friday, 6–0 on three hits on Saturday, and coming back on Monday to win 4–0 on two hits.

In 1910, Johnson's pitching improved markedly. He'd learned batters' weaknesses by this time. He'd also improved his fielding, becoming one of the best in the game. In his twenty-one-year career, he'd go on to have 278 putouts (twelfth best all-time) and 1348 assists (fifth best), to handle the ball 1679 times (fourth best), and to participate in 72 double plays (sixth best).

From 1910 on, Johnson would rack up one league-leading stat after another. He would lead in wins six times. In addition, he registered 20 or more victories twelve times. He led in strikeouts twelves times and is second all-time to Nolan Ryan. And he had more shutouts than anyone six times. His career shutout total of 113 is the highest in baseball history and a record that will probably never be broken.

But the true mark of Johnson's control and domination is his ERA averages. During his first thirteen years, he ran off ERAs of 1.87, 1.64, 2.21, 1.35, 1.89, 1.39, 1.09, 1.72, 1.55, 1.89, 2.30, 1.27, and 1.49. He simply didn't let opposing runners score on his mistakes.

Walter Johnson was everyone's country cousin, big and handsome, pleasant and gentle — with an overpowering fastball. His 416 career wins is the second highest total in baseball history. When asked what accounted for Johnson's success, Chicago White Sox outfielder Ping Bodie answered, "You can't hit what you can't see." Johnson was that fast.

W	L	Pct	ERA	G	GS	GC	IP	H
416	279	.599	2.17	802	666	532	5923.2	4925

Relief Pitching

BB	SO	Sho	W	L	SV
1405	3508	113	42	25	35

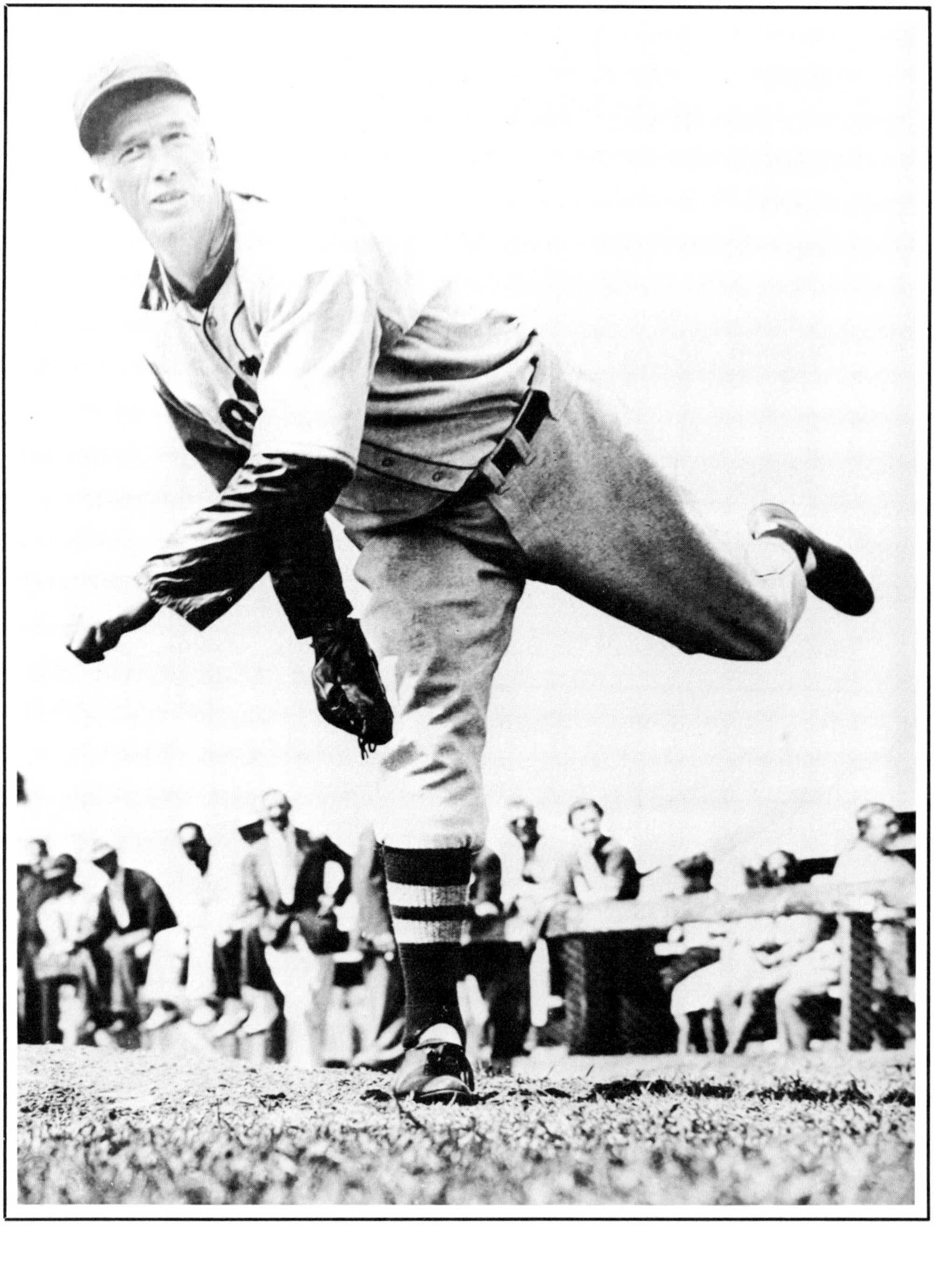

☆ | **PITCHER** | ☆

LEFTY GROVE

Robert Moses Grove (Mose)
Born: May 6, 1900, Lonaconing, Maryland
Died: May 23, 1975, Norwalk, Ohio
Career dates: 1925–1941   Hall of Fame: 1947
Batted and threw left-handed

It was the last of the ninth, and the Philadelphia Athletics held a frail 1–0 lead over the New York Yankees. Pitching for Philadelphia was their six-foot-three fastballer, Lefty Grove.

Mark Koenig led off the inning with a smash to deep right center for a triple. With Koenig just ninety feet away from tying the game, Grove had to face the Yankees' awesome "Murderers' Row" of Ruth, Gehrig, and Bob Meusel.

The fans at Yankee Stadium sat back and waited calmly for the inevitable end. After all, Ruth would hit .356 in 1927, slug 60 home runs, and drive in 164 RBIs. Gehrig's numbers were just as impressive, hitting .373 with 47 homers and 175 RBIs. Even Meusel was solid, with a .337 average and 103 RBIs. No doubt about it, Grove was up against the wall.

But the fans and the Yankees hadn't counted on Grove's fiery determination or his fastball. Grove simply reared back and threw bullets past all three, fanning them on nine straight pitches, with Meusel the only one even to foul a ball off.

Grove was quite simply the fastest thrower of his time and equal in speed to Johnson or Gibson or even modern-day smoke throwers like Goose Gossage or Nolan Ryan.

"Aspirin tablets," a stunned hitter would mumble after facing Grove, "just like aspirin tablets those balls were. . . . I never saw anything like that Grove."

Grove was born and raised in a coal mining town in Maryland. He quit elementary school to work in a silk mill, later finding a better-paying job (at $5.25 a day) in a glass factory. And, of course, he played ball, first in a rutted cow pasture near his home, then for an amateur team in a nearby town.

Word got around about a young kid with a fastball that most catchers couldn't handle, and in short order Grove found himself playing for Jack Dunn's minor league team. Grove would stay with the club five years, winning 108 games and losing only 36. Then Dunn sold him to Philadelphia, and Grove began his major league career in 1925.

Grove's first year was anything but spectacular. He was accustomed to overwhelming minor league batters, intimidating them into swinging blindly at bad pitches. He had never really worked on his control.

Major league batters were more patient and waited on him. Grove came away with a rookie year record of 10–13, a 4.75 ERA, and the booby prize of most walks (131).

In addition to his poor control, Grove's temperament didn't help his pitching performance any. He wasn't petty or demanding like some players. Grove was simply a very ornery guy when he lost. If things began going badly in a game, Grove would take it as a personal insult. He'd get the ball back from the catcher and almost immediately fire it back in. He'd lose his pitching rhythm — and the game.

With the help of catcher Cy Perkins, Grove learned to pace himself between pitches, to think about the batter and where the next pitch should go. Grove would always have a monumental temper — he is noted for destroying a number of clubhouses after close losses — but he always maintained his pitching cool on the mound.

The one bright spot in his first year stats was a league-leading 116 strikeouts. After two seasons of working on his control and temper, Grove emerged as the dominant pitcher of the era.

From 1927 through 1933, Grove won 20 or more games each season, once winning 31. He would lead the league in wins four times, ERA five times, and strikeouts *every* year. Meanwhile, he gave up fewer and fewer walks.

After being traded to the Boston Red Sox in 1934 and sustaining a shoulder injury, Grove developed a good curve to complement his fastball. His strikeout totals dropped somewhat, but he maintained excellent control, winning the ERA title four more times (for a total of nine out of his seventeen seasons).

When he retired in 1941, Grove had 300 wins (he was one of only fifteen pitchers to achieve that number), along with the fourth highest winning percentage.

W	L	Pct	ERA	G	GS	CG	IP	H
300	141	.680	3.06	616	456	300	3940.2	3849

Relief Pitching

BB	SO	Sho	W	L	SV
1187	2266	35	33	22	55

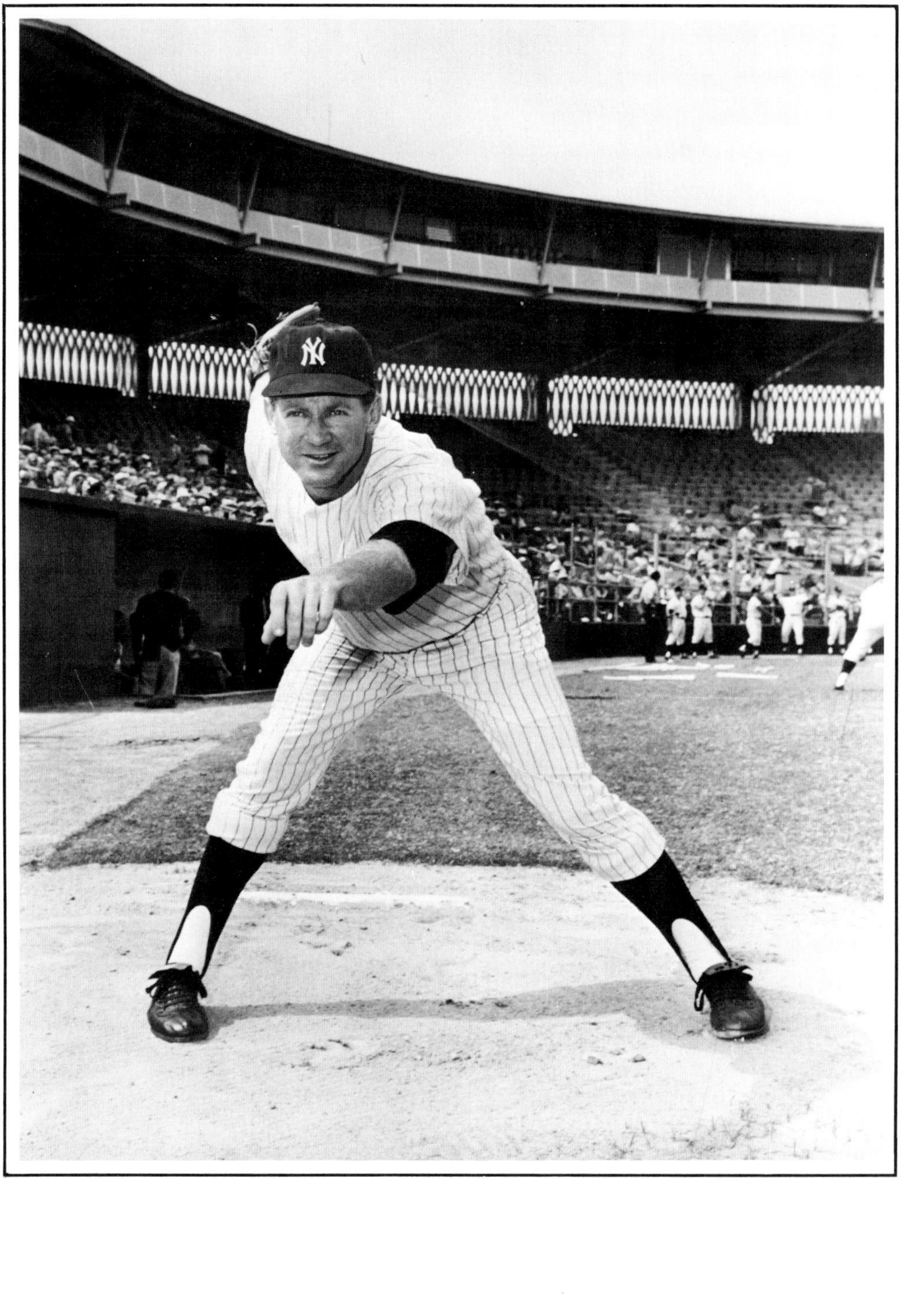

☆ | PITCHER | ☆
WHITEY FORD

Edward Charles Ford (The Chairman of the Board)
Born: October 21, 1928, New York, New York
Career dates: 1950–1967   Hall of Fame: 1974
Batted and threw left-handed

He was known as "The Chairman of the Board," a nickname that describes perfectly the way Whitey Ford dominated the New York Yankee pitching staff and opposing hitters for years.

Ford grew up a typical city kid, playing stickball between the manhole covers in the street and dreaming of being a major league player. This wasn't unusual for a kid from New York City, especially during the Ruth and DiMaggio eras.

The difference between Ford and the other kids was his strong left arm and a phenomenal curve ball. He developed the curve while still in school, practicing for hours to get it to break down and in on right-handed hitters. The 1950 season was already under way when the Yankees, the team Ford had dreamed of playing on, called him up from the minors to help them in their pennant drive.

Ford's first appearance against the Boston Red Sox was anything but auspicious. He came on in relief with the Yanks trailing and proceeded to give up seven hits, six walks, and five runs. "I think we ended up losing seventeen to four, something tidy like that," Ford remembers.

But it wasn't the score that stuck in his mind. It was the way Boston's first-base coach would holler out something to the batters just as Ford was delivering the ball. The next day, after some work in the bullpen, Ford realized that the way he moved his arm while winding up tipped off his pitches. The Boston coach had spotted this and let his players know what was going to be thrown.

Ford immediately set about concealing his pitches. He would stand completely motionless between pitches, concentrating totally on the batter and what he would throw next. Then he'd take a short, businesslike windup (one that never varied no matter what he was going to throw) and snap off the next pitch with efficient quickness. He went on to post a 9–1 record for the remainder of 1950, coming away with a very good 2.81 ERA.

After two years in the army, Ford came back and proved that his rookie record was no fluke. He won 18 and lost just 6 for a .750 winning percentage. Ford accomplished much of this with his curve, of course. It was thrown with pinpoint accuracy and came in a variety of speeds. To really keep batters off stride and guessing, he'd mix in a fastball and, later, a fluttering forkball.

Along the way, Ford also developed one of baseball's best pick-off moves to first. His snappy delivery and left-handedness aided him in this. Runners had very little time to react, and Ford was always facing toward first base. As a result, runners stayed close to the bag when Ford was on the mound. This cut out most hit-and-run attempts and reduced the runs scored against him.

It all seemed to work very well for Ford. Only once in his sixteen years did he give up more hits than innings pitched, and he had sub-3.00 ERAs eleven times. He wasn't known as a strikeout artist, but his total of 1956 strikeouts ranks sixteenth all-time.

The bottom line on Ford is that he was a consistent winner. His lifetime mark of 236 wins, 106 loses, is good for a .690 winning percentage, tying him with Dave Foutz for the best ever in that category. Maybe even more important, in sixteen seasons of hurling, Ford helped get the Yankees into eleven World Series!

W	L	Pct	ERA	G	GS	CG	IP	H
236	106	.690	2.75	498	438	156	3170.1	2766

Relief Pitching

BB	SO	Sho	W	L	SV
1086	1956	45	9	7	10

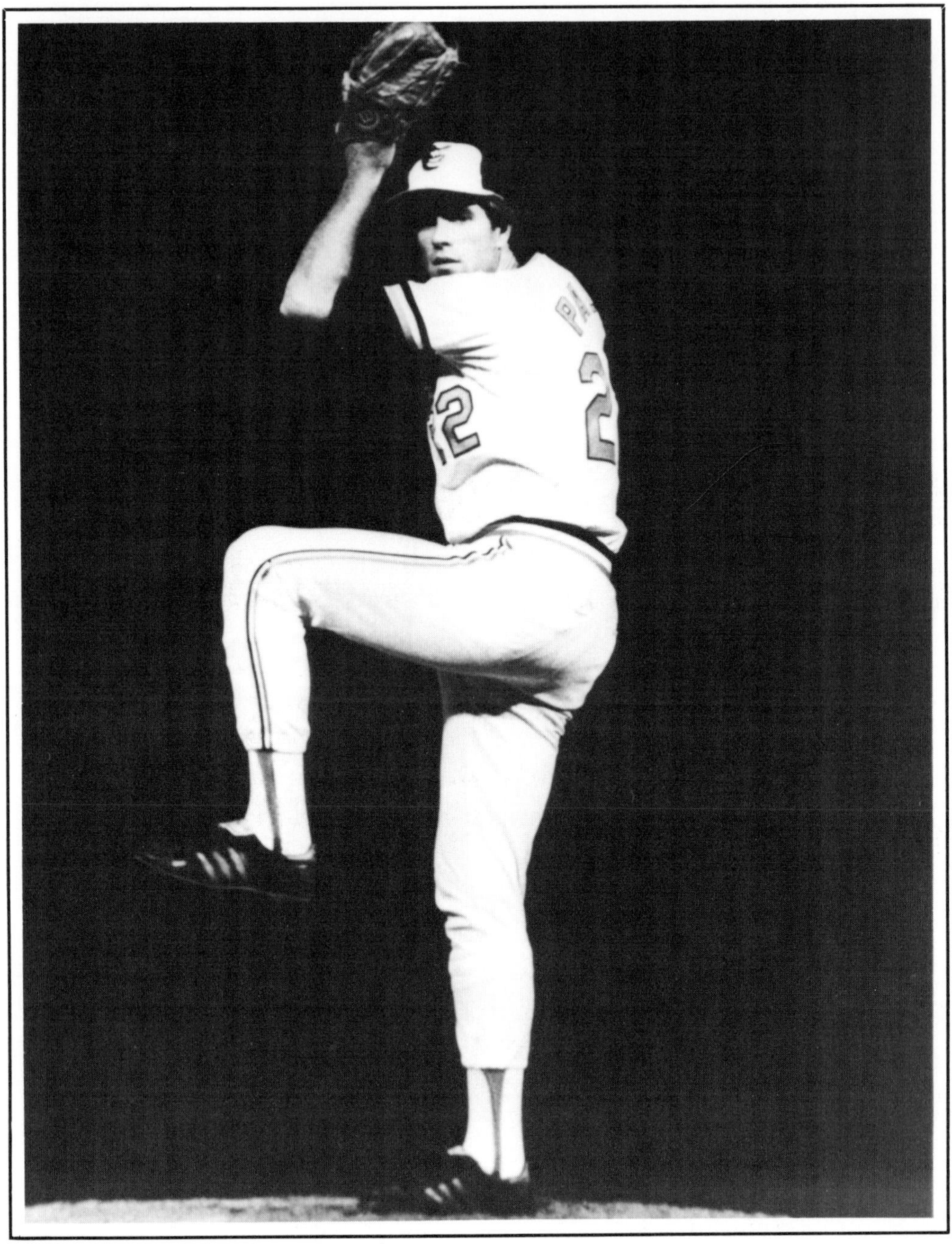

☆ PITCHER ☆
JIM PALMER

James Alvin Palmer
Born: October 15, 1945, New York, New York
Career dates: 1965–
Bats and throws right-handed

Control. That was Jim Palmer's main goal when he entered a game. If he maintained perfect control of his pitches, he'd control the batters — and the game. This single-mindedness made Palmer one of the premier pitchers of his era and led to some notable confrontations with one of his managers, Earl Weaver.

"Oh, we went at it a couple of times there," Weaver has recalled somewhat fondly. They usually "went at it" when Weaver felt his star pitcher was laboring and had to come out of the game. If Palmer felt he was being taken out prematurely, he'd argue his case with Weaver even as the reliever approached the mound. Then he'd argue with Weaver in the dugout, in the clubhouse after the game, and sometimes for days afterward. While Palmer's combative nature sometimes seemed comical, it revealed his unfailing belief in his ability to control any pitching situation no matter how bad it might seem to others. It was a belief he had to form shortly after he joined the Baltimore Orioles in 1965.

Why? The Baltimore team was a hodgepodge of talent. It was made up of older players who were effective, but well past their prime, and younger players who either hadn't rounded into major league form or were pathetic hitters. The team would be inconsistent in its run production, so Palmer knew he had to hold opponents to a run or two and hope for the best. Palmer's first year was spent in relief mostly, and he came away with a 5–4 record.

In Palmer's second year he joined the starting rotation and had a strong 15–10 record, accomplished in large part by a sizzling fastball that jumped up as it neared the plate. But while his win-lose record was solid, his ERA was high at 3.46.

Palmer's problem was a common one, especially for pitchers who feel they must be perfect to make up for their less than perfect team. If he found himself down by a run, Palmer would aim his pitches, trying to nick the corners and get batters on called strike threes. But a pitcher doing this will usually take something off the ball to attain such control, and reduced speed makes the ball move less as it approaches the plate. The result, of course, is more hits and runs.

A shoulder injury caused Palmer to spend much of 1967 and 1968 in the minors, but when he came back in 1969, he'd learned to relax. He threw with ease and confidence and didn't try too hard to be perfect in placement of the ball. He posted an impressive 16–4 record, with a sharp 2.34 ERA. He gave up fewer walks and hits, while striking out 123 batters. Six of his wins were shutouts, an indication of control and effectiveness.

Palmer would go on to win 20 or more games eight times, while posting the lowest career ERA for any American League pitcher since 1920. He ranks twentieth in winning percentage, fifteenth in shutouts, and thirty-third in strikeouts. His ability to keep runners off the base can be seen in the seventeenth lowest ratio of hits per nine innings; he gave up only 7.56.

After the 1981 season, Palmer set his sights on the magic 300 win mark, a feat accomplished by only fifteen pitchers in baseball history. The thirty-eight-year-old hurler would post a 15–5 record in 1982, only to miss most of 1983 because of back and shoulder problems. Knowing that time was fast running out for him unless he could once again regain control, Palmer put aside pride and voluntarily went down to the minors to pitch himself back into top form. It's just this sort of "take control of the situation" attitude that has made Palmer the pitcher he is — and led to his squabbles with Weaver. Yet despite their often volatile relationship, Weaver's analysis of Palmer's pitching ability is to the point: "He's a Hall of Fame pitcher."

W	L	Pct	ERA	G	GS	CG	IP	H
267	149	.636	2.89	548	517	212	3953.2	3361

			Relief Pitching		
BB	SO	Sho	W	L	SV
1330	2221	51	7	2	4

But What About...

"Sure, these are all great players," a reader might say, "but what about Roberto Clemente? Now, he was super. Every bit as good as Aaron!" Others might wonder about Rod Carew or Joe DiMaggio or Pete Rose or Jimmie Foxx or. . . .

The amazing thing about baseball is that it has always attracted many of America's greatest athletes. Each generation has produced a score of outstanding players and a handful of true superstars. And fans from each generation tend to proclaim the players they actually saw in action as the best. It's understandable. Anyone who's seen a Brooks Robinson diving catch at third can't imagine any other human being so quick or agile or sure-handed. That is, until they run into another fan who happened to be around during Pie Traynor's days.

In choosing these twenty-six players, I've tried to be as impartial and as thorough as possible. But in the end, this list, like any other such list, has to be personal to some extent. If your favorite player doesn't appear here, don't be upset. Instead, do a little legwork — get some books out of the library, gather facts, and try to form an accurate picture of your player's all-around game. Who knows? You might build a strong case for getting that player on one of *Baseball's All-Time All-Star* teams.

Bibliography

A *Baseball Century*. New York: Rutledge Books, Macmillan Publishing Co., 1976.
Allen, Lee. *The National League Story*. New York: Hill and Wang, 1961.
Angell, Roger. *Five Seasons*. New York: Simon and Schuster, 1977.
Angell, Roger. *Late Innings: A Baseball Companion*. New York: Simon and Schuster, 1982.
Appel, Martin, and Burt Goldblatt. *Baseball's Best*. New York: McGraw-Hill, 1976.
Cohen, Richard, Jordon Deutsch, Roland Johnson, and David Neft. *The Sports Encyclopedia: Baseball*. New York: Grosset and Dunlap, 1974.
Creamer, Robert. *Babe*. New York: Simon and Schuster, 1974.
Dickey, Glenn. *The History of the American League: Since 1901*. Briarcliff Manor, N.Y.: A Scarborough Book, Stein and Day Publishers, 1980.
Dickey, Glenn. *The History of the National League: Since 1976*. Briarcliff Manor, N.Y.: A Scarborough Book, Stein and Day Publishers, 1982.
Hertzel, Bob. *The Big Red Machine*. Englewood Cliffs, N.J.: Prentice-Hall, 1976.
James, Bill. *The Bill James Baseball Abstract*. New York: Ballantine Books, 1983.
Klein, Larry. "Bill Dickey: Baseball's Immortal Catcher." *Sport* magazine, July 1961.
Koufax, Sandy, and Ed Linn. *Koufax*. New York: Viking Press, 1966.
Lau, Charley. *The Art of Hitting .300*. New York: Hawthorne Press, 1980.
Libby, Bill. "The Sophistication of Sandy Koufax." *Sport* magazine, September 1963.
Linn, Ed. "Ted Williams: The Kid's Last Game." *Sport* magazine, February 1961.
Mathewson, Christy. *Pitching in a Pinch*. New York: Stein and Day Publishers, 1977.
Meany, Tom. *Baseball's Greatest Pitchers*. Cranbury, N.J.: A. S. Barnes & Co., 1951.
Reichler, Joseph L. *The Great All-Time Baseball Record Book*. New York: Macmillan Publishing Co., 1981.

Reichler, Joseph L., editor. *The Baseball Encyclopedia*, 5th edition. New York: Macmillan Publishing Co., 1982.

Ritter, Lawrence, and Donald Honig. *The 100 Greatest Baseball Players of All Time*. New York: Crown Publishers, 1981.

Shapiro, Milton. *The Hank Aaron Story*. New York: Julian Messner, 1961.

Tharn, John. *Baseball's Dream Team*. New York: Tempo Books, Grosset and Dunlap, 1982.

INDEX

Page numbers in *italics* refer to photographs.

Aaron, Hank, 5, 26, 31, 33–36, *35*, 96, 114
Abbreviations for statistics, 4
Alexander, Grover Cleveland, 5, *40*, 41–43, 45, 53
All-Star games, 2
Athletics, Philadelphia, 65, 95, 103, 104

Baker, Frank (Home Run), 100
Barons, Birmingham, 29
Barrow, Ed, 79
Baseball Writers Association, 69
Bench, Johnny, 5, 37–39, 75, 92
Berra, Yogi, 92–94
Billingham, Jack, 33, 36
Bluege, Ossie, 69
Bodie, Ping, 101
Bouchee, Ed, 31
Braves, Atlanta, 33, 36
Braves, Boston, 81

Cantillon, Jon, 99–100
Cardinals, St. Louis, 13–15, 51

Carew, Rod, 114
Carlton, Steve, 56
Carrigan, Bill, 78
Chesbro, Jack, 95
Choosing the players, basis for, 1–3, 114
Clemente, Roberto, 31, 52, 114
Cobb, Ty, 2, 5, 15, 29, 34, 45, 82, 83–85, 99, 100
Collins, Eddie, 5, *64*, 65–67
Crawford, Wahoo Sam, 100
Cronin, Joe, 5, 23, *68*, 69–71
Crowder, General, 69
Cubs, Chicago, 42, 50
Cy Young Award, 2

Derringer, Paul, 92
Dickey, Bill, 5, 38, 91–94, *93*,
DiMaggio, Joe, 29, 62, 107, 114
Dodgers, Brooklyn, 49
Downing, Al, 36
Dunn, Jack, 77, 104

Ely, Bones, 16

| 117

INDEX

"Fadeaway," 45, 46
Forbes Field, Chicago, 81
Ford, Whitey, 5, 78, *106*, 107–09
Foutz, Dave, 109
Foxx, Jimmy, 114

Gehrig, Lou, 5, *60*, 61–63, 80, 103
Giants, New York, 9–11, 14, 18, 30, 31, 45, 80
Giants, San Francisco, 38
Gibson, Bob, 3, 5, 42, 51–*53*, 56, 95, 103
Golden Glove Award, 2, 3, 38, 52, 74
Gomez, Lefty, 16
Gossage, Goose, 103
Grove, Lefty, 5, *102*, 103–05

Hall of Fame, 2, 9, 13, 16, 19, 21, 24, 29, 33, 41, 45, 49, 51, 61, 65, 69, 73, 77, 83, 87, 91, 95, 99, 103, 107, 113
Haney, Fred, 33–34
Harris, Bucky, 63
Helms, Tommy, 75
Hornsby, Rogers, 5, 10, *12*, 13–15, 33, 34, 88
Howard, Elston, 94
Huggins, Miller, 61–62, 91, 94

Jackson, Reggie, 22, 80
Johnson, Judy, 3
Johnson, Walter, 5, 95, *98*, 99–101, 103

Kerr, Dickie, 24
Koenig, Mark, 103
Koufax, Sandy, 5, *48*, 49–50, 51, 95
Kuhn, Bowie, 36

Leonard, Buck, 3
Lolich, Mickey, 96

McClary, Socko, 70
McGraw, John, 9–10, 18
Mack, Connie, 65
Maranville, Rabbit, 21
Mathewson, Christy, 5, *44*, 45–47, 95
Matthews, Gary, 38
Mays, Willie, 5, *28*, 29–32, 34, 79
Mets, New York, 55, 56, 100
Meusel, Bob, 103
Most Valuable Player Award, 2
Most Valuable Player Award, World Series, 38
Musial, Stan, 5, 24–27, *25*, 34

Negro Leagues, 3, 29–30

Orioles, Baltimore, 73, 111–12

Paige, Satchel, 3
Palmer, Jim, 5, *110*, 111–13
Perkins, Cy, 104
Phillies, Philadelphia, 41, 42
Pipp, Wally, 62
Pirates, Pittsburgh, 16, 19, 21, 23, 52, 70
Plank, Eddie, 5, 95–96, *97*
Polo Grounds, New York, 80

Red Sox, Boston, 69, 71, 77, 78, 87, 105, 107
Reds, Cincinnati, 37, 38, 46–47, 56, 74–75
Rickey, Branch, 13, 14–15
Rigney, Bill, 30
Robinson, Brooks, 5, 22, *72*, 73–75, 114
Robinson, Jackie, 29–30

INDEX

Rogers Hornsby Baseball School, 15
Rookie of the Year Award, 30, 55
Rose, Pete, 52, 75, 114
Roth, Braggo, 78
Ruth, Babe, 5, 31, 33, 34, 36, 62, 63, 76, 77–81, 103, 107
Ryan, Nolan, 50, 100–01, 103

Screwball, 46
Seaver, Tom, 5, 54, 55–57, 100
Senators, Washington, 69, 70, 71, 99, 100
Shortstop of the Year, 69
Sisler, George, 10
Speaker, Tris, 26
Statistics, 1–2, 4
Stoneham, Charles, 80

Team rosters, 5
Terry, Bill, 5, 8, 9–11, 23

Thompson, Bobby, 33
Tigers, Detroit, 83
Traynor, Pie, 5, 20, 21–23, 74, 114

Wagner, Honus, 5, 16–19, 17
Weaver, Earl, 111, 113
Webb, Earl, 69
Wertz, Vic, 31
Williams, Ted, 5, 86, 87–90
Wilson, Hack, 12
Wood, Smokey Joe, 96
World Series, 2, 31, 37, 38, 56, 62, 74–75, 78, 92, 109

Yankee Stadium, New York, 80, 103
Yankees, New York, 61, 79–81, 91, 92–94, 100, 103, 107, 109
Young, Cy, 2, 95